BONES OF CONTENTION

BONES OF CONTENTION

A Popular Consideration of Sublime Topics
For Use by Catholics Over Beer and Pretzels

Fr. John D. Bolderson
Priest by the Grace of God
Ph.D. by Twist of Irony

Queenship

PUBLISHING COMPANY
P.O. Box 220 • Goleta, CA 93116
(800) 647-9882 • (805) 692-0043 • Fax: (805) 967-5843

Nihil Obstat:
Reverend Msgr. William J. Blacet, J.C.L.
Censor Deputatus

Imprimatur:
Most Reverend Raymond J. Boland, D.D.
Bishop of Kansas City-St. Joseph
December 11, 2000

Library of Congress Number # 20-01130160 → 200113016 0

Published by:
Queenship Publishing
P.O. Box 220
Goleta, CA 93116
(800) 647-9882 • (805) 692-0043 • Fax: (805) 967-5843

Printed in the United States of America

ISBN: 1-57918-171-6 →978-1-57918-171-0

Call # - BX1747.B65 2001

Table of Contents

For the best reasons I can think of for
being Proud to be a priest:

Fr. Brian Driscoll
Fr. Larry Huber
Fr. Jeff Maassen
Fr. Jim Taranto

Introduction

This little book is the continuation of a number of conversations about things that are important to Catholics. It includes ideas about such subjects as inclusive language, capital punishment, Marian dogmas, clerical celibacy, the forgiveness of sins, marriage, the ordination of men, and ecumenism. Some of these issues are hotly contested, and cause pain. I hope that I have not added to that. I respect all well-thought-out opinions, including those that contradict my own. A person can be wrong without being stupid. Perhaps at a later time there may be more *bones of contention,* expressing some of those positions. I would like to see that.

Generally, I have tried to limit my concerns to things that might be discussed at a backyard barbecue or Friday night card game. I have not attempted to give anything close to a final word on any of these subjects, and I have never claimed to be even handed on any of these issues. I am absolutely and unabashedly proud of my Church, its institutions, and its teachings. I have approached them in a respectful but lighthearted way, often using simple stories to make my point.

A person or a group of people, who have had a major effect on my life, has inspired each part of this book. I am filled with gratitude for these friends and family members, God has given me, to sustain me with love.

It is my hope, that the thoughts, that I have presented here, will be the beginnings of many more discussions. It has always been my experience, that such conversations go better with pretzels and cold beer.

BONE 1

Inclusive Language

The Three Guys I Admire Most,
The Father, Son, and Holy Ghost,
Took the Last Train for the Coast

For nearly two thousand years, the Church has wrestled with language to adequately explain the mystery of God. At the end of the second century, Tertullian invented a non-biblical way of speaking about the mystery of God, by identifying God as a *Unity in Trinity.* The relation of the Father to the Son and Spirit he later described as one of Personhood. Thus, he proclaimed the one God, a Trinity of Persons.

The implication is that we, who are made in the *Image and Likeness of God,* are most reflective of the Divine Image when we are part of a community of persons, united in love. Therefore, the pattern and end of all human interactions is the Trinity.

The Trinity is not a static reality, like a pound of ground chuck. It is a relationship in dynamic motion. The Father is approached, through the Son, in the Holy Spirit. The ultimate Christian prayer, the Eucharist, is always in that kind of motion. When it becomes a one-sided conversation between an individual and a generic, plain-label God, it goes nowhere; is directed nowhere; accomplishes nothing; and is as dead and lifeless as our lump of ground meat.

With that in mind, I made my way to a convent of religious women, composed of members of different religious orders. One of the sisters invited me to be the celebrant of the community Eucharist. She said, "I think that the sisters will enjoy your gifts."

A more unaware Daniel never entered the lion's den with greater naïve innocence.

I began the mass in the usual way. The Sign of the Cross was followed with the opening greeting, "The Lord be with you."

The response was somewhat unexpected, "And *God* be with you!"

It was really more of a battle cry than a response. I knew that I was in trouble.

The rest of the mass went that way. Every time I began the usual dialogue with the sisters before me, my non-inclusive language was corrected. *Lord* was rendered *God. Father* was rendered *God.* At times I could not tell if we were addressing the Father or the Son or the Spirit. The thought occurred to me that a Unitarian would be comfortable joining us in prayer.

Finally, I invited the sisters to pray the prayer that Jesus taught us. I braced myself for whatever the opening words of the *Lord's Prayer* might be.

The sisters began, "Heavenly Progenitor...."

That did it! I committed the unforgivable sin. I laughed—not long. The silence that followed impressed upon me the hostility that I had earned. Nothing was funny from then on.

Upon reflection, I doubt that I would have minded the sisters praying in the way they did if I had been made aware of it before beginning the liturgy. Perhaps, they were unaware of the hostility in their voices. In any event, I wanted nothing more than to assist them in praying together. I was not there to correct them, or resist them in any way. I was simply caught off guard, and reacted badly. Nevertheless, their insistence upon inclusive language motivated me to rethink the way that the Church speaks about God.

Because I am a product of the Latin West, I use male terminology, exclusively, when referring to the Mystery of the Trinity. *Pater*, Father, is a male Latin noun. *Filius,* Son, is also male. *Spiritus Sanctus,* Holy Spirit, is another masculine term. The words for the Persons of the Trinity are all male words in the Latin tradition.

It is not so in the Greek tradition. Greeks use masculine words when speaking of the Father and the Son, but a neuter term, Hagia

Sophia, is used for the Holy Spirit. *He,* the Father, and *He,* the Son are co-equal with *It,* the Holy Spirit, or Holy Wisdom.

Nor is it so in the Syriac tradition. In this Jewish branch of Christianity, now divided into the various Syriac rites of the Catholic and Orthodox Churches, the Trinity is spoken of in terms of *He,* the Father, *He,* the Son, and *She,* the Spirit. In this implied theology, the Holy Spirit is the eternal *Mother* of the *Eternal Son.* The obvious difficulty, of assigning a role to Mary in this system, was simply not addressed.

Latin Christianity was a *law.* Greek Christianity was a *wisdom.* Syriac Christianity was a *life.* Lived Christianity did not have to be quite as tidy as legal or philosophical Christianity. Mary could remain the human mother of God in history, while the Eternal Mother of the Word maintained Her divine place in the Eternal Trinity. Thus, not only was the Trinity a loving community of Divine Persons, it was an Eternal Family. If the Father was eternally the Father, and the Son was eternally the Son, who else could be the eternal Mother? Certainly, She could not be Mary. Mary was a creature. She had a beginning in human time. She was not present for all eternity. There was simply no other *Person* eternally there, other than the Spirit.

I fully realize that God has no concrete gender. The human words used to describe the indescribable are limited symbols used to express something of the unlimited. I have honestly tried to picture God without gender. The problem is that I have never known a person without a specific gender. Frankly, I am unable to picture any person without casting him or her in those terms. I have the same problem when attempting to picture the Father without gender. I end up thinking of a bright light or a billowing cloud or even the raw power of nature. I think of their purity and power. However, I find it impossible to establish any kind of personal relationship with them. I quite simply feel no love for a light, cloud, or energy, nor am I able to believe in any love returning from them. Despite the contemporary mantra, *God has no gender*, I find myself agreeing with Jesus, who finds it easier to speak to God as *Father.*

Nevertheless, the recognition that one of the original branches of Christianity included femininity in the Trinity legitimizes the continued search for words that more clearly express who God is in every age for people who find little comfort in traditional terminology. It is perfectly acceptable to attempt to find other words in the living tradition of the Church to make the mystery of God more meaningful for all of the people.

However, it is vital to maintain the dynamic character of the Trinity. Every prayer is directed to the Father, through the Son, in the Spirit. When Christians obscure that reality, nothing else in our faith makes any sense.

Some pitfalls have to be avoided when searching for new Trinitarian language. Functionalism destroys the relation among the Divine Persons in the Trinity. *Father, Son,* and *Holy Spirit* express identity. *Creator, Redeemer,* and *Sanctifier* express function. Creator no more captures the Personhood of the Father, than *chief cook and bottle washer* captures the personhood of wife and mother, or than *bread winner* expresses husband and father, especially when the wife may, in fact, be the primary wage earner for the family. Redeemer and Sanctifier are no more expressive of Divine Personhood than Creator.

Functionalism actually denies personhood. The *nurse* will be in later, and will give me my medication. The *state trooper* pulled me over. The *teacher* assigned a ten-page paper. It such cases, *nurse, state trooper,* or *teacher* does not express who that person is. Those terms indicate what the three people do, but not how they differ from the long list of other people, who happen to share their same occupations.

If someone asks me, "Who is that woman?" and they are referring to a picture of my mother, I identify her by saying, "My mom." That expresses more than what she did in life. Being my mother was not her job or function. She was not the sum total of the things she did in life. She was greater than that. She had an identity. She was a person. For me, *mom* expresses that personhood perfectly. She was *mom* when she held me, and took care of me. She was also *mom* when she was in a hospital bed, in a coma, and unable to do anything. I had a relationship with the person. I sometimes describe the things that she did, but they were not her. Her identity, her personhood, was a mystery that I was only allowed to approach by loving her and knowing that she loved me.

The Persons who make up the Trinity can only be intimately known in the same way. Every paragraph of the Eucharistic Prayer begins with the word, *Father*, or *Lord*, which is shown to mean *Father* by its context. This is not simply a matter of gender overkill. If the mass is not a matter of personal contact between the believer and God, it is of little value. God is not a thing, a lump of stone, wood, or metal. God is a Community, perhaps even a Family, of Persons.

The process that is supposed to take place, when experiencing this mystery, is identified by the Greek name for the mass, Eucharist. The word means *Thanksgiving*. It is a Greek rendering of the Hebrew word *baracha*, which is usually understood as *blessing*. Jews bless, or thank, God for something He has given them. Christian worship is also a matter of thanking God. We come together to thank the Father for giving us life, through the Son. The prayer is a miraculous mystery made possible by the Holy Spirit. For when we thank God for sending His Son to us, the Son, by that very act of gratitude, becomes present on our altars. Entering into this mystery is an encounter with the Trinity. It is made possible by following the Person of the Son to the Father. All of this is accomplished through the action of the Person of the Holy Spirit, who dwells in His people, making them greater than the sum total of their number.

The Eucharist is intimate. It is a contact between persons, granted not equal persons, but persons. It is also vital for the human persons who go to, through, and in the Father, the Son and the Holy Spirit, to see in those around them an opportunity to reflect the great Trinitarian mystery that they enter into at every celebration of the mass.

No one can ever really go to God alone. The Christian never begins the *Lord's Prayer* by saying, "*My* Father who art in heaven...." Even when we are completely alone, the Son has taught us to enter into the mystery of prayer by saying, "*Our* Father."

Blessing the Father, for his gift of the Son, changes the bread and wine into the Person, for whom we have come together, to thank the Father. We come bearing a gift for the Almighty God, who has made everything, and who needs nothing. Our Christian worship is a matter of offering to the Father the Son that He has already given to us. The love we have for one another, when we present this Divine offering, makes us the most perfect reflection of the Image and Likeness of God possible for mere creatures to attain.

Christian Tradition is alive. Static human words can never fully capture the meaning of any Divine Mystery. New terms come into use. Understanding makes progress without destroying all that has already been discovered. In this development, human culture is neutral. It provides the soil in which the truth takes root.

The indwelling of the Holy Spirit allows new ways of speaking about the Trinity that take into account the part of the *Image and Likeness of God* that happens to be female. They are valid, as long as they convey the unity of the Divine Persons, the Trinity, and the entering into the life of that mystery through dynamic prayer. Anything else would be less than dead. It would be totally unapproachable, and completely meaningless for the entire human race.

Through Him, with Him, and in Him, in the Unity of the Holy Spirit, all glory and honor are yours, Almighty Father, forever and ever. Amen!

BONE 2

The Death Penalty

The Pastoral Visit of Pope John Paul II
St. Louis — 30 January 1999

As I sat before the Holy Father in the Trans World Dome, I expected little that would change my thinking or alter the way that I go through life. He was one of my heroes. He had risked his life for the Gospel, under Nazi and Communist dictators. He had been prepared to place his body in front of invading Russian tanks on the boarder of his homeland. This holy athlete had sacrificed his health and vigor for the Church. He had survived an attempted assassination and offered himself as a replacement for hostages. He deserved to be heard, even when he said difficult things. I already agreed with him on just about everything he would say, except for capital punishment.

I had always considered myself pro-life. The concept that all human life is a sacred gift from God, and, therefore, *innocent* human life could never be taken, made perfect sense to me. Perhaps because I was a former U.S. Marine, thorny areas, like war or capital punishment, seemed to fall slightly outside the area of *innocent* human life. Surely, the concept of self-defense covered war, and with a bit of a stretch, so did capital punishment. Didn't the state have the right to protect its citizens from serial murderers and other predators?

I had difficulty with facile arguments that suggested that the state was just as bad as a mass murderer when it executed someone

7

who had tortured and murdered numerous innocent people. How could the state be as evil as Jeffery Dahmer if it took his life for what he had done? How could a painless shot of poison, to an unconscious cannibal, be equated with the fiendish horror that he had inflicted on so many boys and men? To be just as bad as Jeffery Dahmer, the state would have to bring him back to life, dozens of times, and then kill him, with the same terror and pain that he had inflicted on his victims. Then the state would have to serve up Dahmer stew in the state prison. It was impossible for the state to be as bad as Jeffery Dahmer, at least to Dahmer.

Was it possible to take a life to proclaim its value? It seemed to me, that someone who had done the unimaginable could forfeit the right to breathe the same air that he had denied to his victims. Couldn't society say: *You have behaved like an animal. You have degraded human life by your conscious choice. Killing you tells the entire world that we will not allow anyone to treat innocent human victims with your kind of brutality and uncivilized callousness. Human life is too sacred to allow you to live after what you have done.*

I was aware of the position of the American bishops. Cardinal Bernadine had used the seamless garment of Jesus to stress the necessity of a unified life ethic for believers. The Holy Father had moved the Church further away from the death penalty than any previous pope. But there still remained the escape clause. The state was not absolutely prohibited from taking the life of a monstrous criminal, in exceptional circumstances.

Then the pope came to St. Louis, and everything changed, at least for me. I did not hear the Holy Father say that nations *could not* take the lives of notorious criminals. I heard him say that the state *should not* use this cruel and unnecessary remedy for society's ills. I did not hear a defense of the criminal. I heard a defense of the Church's mission. People who commit horrible acts of violence, even inhuman acts of cruel degradation, can not be converted if they are dead. *Conversion*, that is the mission of the Church. God does not want the death of a sinner. He wants conversion.

The state has its job: to protect its citizens. The Church has its job: to lead sinners to repentance and change. If the state does its job in a way that prevents the Church from carrying out its mission, the Church is conscience-bound to request that the state get out of its way.

Of course, the Church has no power to force the state to do anything. It shouldn't even enter into an argument over the relative justice or injustice of execution. The Church readily proclaims that society has the right to defend itself from violent and dangerous people. But the Church does want the chance to convince even the cruelest among us that they have ignored the human dignity of their victims. It wishes to have the opportunity to convict the murderer in his own heart. It wants to bring the light of human compassion into the soul of a monster, so that he can discover everything that he has denied. The Church wants the killer to feel the love of the God that he has done all that he could to negate, through his evil actions. The Church wants the chance to convince the murderer that a convicted criminal, Jesus, was executed by the state, to atone for his sins too. Once the worst of sinners has understood and faced the full impact of his crime, he can begin to approach the grandeur of God's forgiveness and love. That conversion is the ultimate proclamation of the sacredness of my own human life.

Perhaps, such a person should never be free to repeat his descent into inhumanity. That may be a way of pointing out how evil his actions were. The state is human. It will never be able to forgive as God forgives; maybe, it shouldn't even try. The Church, on the other hand, is both human and divine. It struggles with its human, sometimes vengeful, heart and its divine mission. Perhaps, that is why it took a visit from the Holy Father to awaken, in this pro-life heart, the rejection of the ultimate denial of conversion.

I am alive and can change. Those on death row should be given the same opportunity—not because they deserve it, they most certainly do not! Nevertheless, the Church must continue to try to spread the truth of God's mercy to all human beings, even those made the most undeserving by their own inhuman actions.

Church and state are separate in this country. That is the way most of us want it. Still, the Church has a voice and must be free to state its opinion. Sometimes the state listens, and sometimes it does not. That has nothing to do with the mandate the Church has to proclaim its message.

Human life is sacred. It is a gift from God, and belongs to God. It is not the private property of the recipient, the parent, or the state. It remains sacred even when declared outside the protection of the law. It is still sacred when the murderer steals it. It is sacred when the state takes it in a *humane* and painless way. It is sacred when twisted logic attempts a compassionate appeal for its end. This is so even if the Church has a less than perfect record in fulfilling its mission to proclaim its dignity for the *slave, heretic,* or *infidel.* It is so, even if the state never recognizes it. It will always be so!

Thank you, Holy Father, for the reminder.

BONE 3

Mary

**A woman clothed with the sun,
And the moon under her feet,
And upon her head a crown of twelve stars**

The Foundation

In the second century, a young priest left Syria for missionary activity in what would one day become France. Upon his arrival, he made his way to the local arena. A persecution of religious nonconformists had broken out. Gnostics, Christians, and some of the more exotic forms of paganism had been identified as harmful to the body politic.

To his horror he watched as those helpless people were tortured to death. One woman, Blandina, was placed in a sack and thrown to a wild bull. A gentle giant of a man, Attalus, was paraded around the stadium with a contemptuous sign around his neck proclaiming that he was a Christian. He was then stripped and forced to sit in a metal chair that had been heated, white hot.

The young priest smelled the burning flesh, endured the screams of agony, and saw the blood of those people as it was splashed around the arena for the entertainment of the laughing crowd.

As he observed the martyrdom of his brothers and sisters, the priest listened to the taunts of the mob. "Who are these people? What do they believe? Why are they dying?"

The young Syrian priest, Irenaeus, determined that never again would Christians die, and the world not know why. He left that stadium, and began work on his *Against Heresies*. This was the first systematic attempt to identify the doctrines of those who believed in Jesus Christ.

He began the story where one might expect, with the creation of the human race. Adam and Eve began their lives in Paradise. They chose to turn their backs on God, and sin entered the world.

Jesus was God's way of correcting what the first people had done. The human race got a second chance. Jesus was a new Adam. Mankind could start all over again. There were two *in the beginnings*, one at the dawn of creation, recorded in Genesis; the other at the emergence of redemption, found at the beginning of John's Gospel. This second chance for the human race was called, *Recapitulation*. It was about who Jesus was, and what he meant to every human being who would ever live. But if Jesus was the new Adam, who could be the new Eve?

The answer, without being too literal on this point, was Mary. She was the exact antithesis of Eve. Eve became the mother of the human race through the loss of her virginity. Mary would become the mother of believers as a perpetual virgin. Eve became the mother of man. Mary would become the mother of God. Eve was the original sinner. Mary would be untouched by sin from the first moment of her conception. Eve invited sickness, death, and decay into the world, and returned to the earth from which she and her husband had been made. Mary would be totally untouched by corruption. She would be assumed into heaven.

All that the Church would have to say, over the next two thousand years, about Mary, would rest, at least partially, upon this original insight of Irenaeus that Mary was the new Eve.

The Four Marian Dogmas

The number and variety of Marian devotions, practiced by members of the Catholic Church, are impossible to estimate, with any meaningful accuracy. Popular statues and paintings, pilgrimage destinations, apparitions, dancing suns, changing rosaries, healing waters, secret messages, and endless localized customs and miraculous stories comprise a popular religiosity that is astounding in its creativity and diversity. Mary has been pictured as a member of nearly every race and nationality.

The Catholic Church has always promoted the cult of Mary. At the same time, it has always been somewhat uncomfortable with the aspects of Marian devotion that lend themselves to uncontrollable emotional outbursts. In extreme cases, the Church has been embarrassed by some of the more exotic expressions of popular Marian piety. However, in every age, Mary has been used by the Church to say profound things about Jesus and the economy of salvation. In fact, Marian dogmas constitute a kind of shorthand for proclaiming some of the more profound teachings of the Church.

There are four great Marian dogmas: Ever Virgin, Mother of God, the Immaculate Conception, and the Assumption. The first of these concerns the Perpetual Virginity of Mary. The entire point of a dogma is that it is a belief so central to Christianity that to refuse to acknowledge it is to place one's self outside of the community of believers. The very act of definition is an admission that a particular teaching is not explicitly found in Sacred Scripture. If it were, why would further elaboration be necessary? An explicit teaching, found in the bible, would be impossible to deny; it would not be open for controversy. Nevertheless, because a dogma is of necessity part of the original truth of Divine Revelation, it has to be at least implied in Sacred Scripture.

Ever Virgin

At present, every mass begins with a penitential rite. Mary *Ever Virgin* is called upon to pray for the repentant sinner. Nevertheless, if one were to ask the people leaving mass if they believed that Mary was a virgin before, during, and forever after the birth of Jesus, the variety of answers might equal the forms of devotion already mentioned.

Among all of the people of the world, Catholics seem unique in their ability to say things that mean absolutely nothing at all to those who say them. This is a learned skill. It ranks up there with the ability to listen to a proclamation of a bible passage at mass and then completely forget what was read minutes before. I have often asked worshipers at mass if they remembered the name of the first reading, or the second reading, or the gospel. It is astounding how few people have the ability to remember what was proclaimed less than five minutes earlier.

It takes years to develop this kind of talent. One starts in infancy, when successfully attending mass means not screaming too loudly or too long. It continues in childhood, when one sits, motionless and glassy eyed, while things are being said that can not possibly register as coherent thoughts. It makes progress though adolescence when the words are understandable, but they simply do not match new feelings and interests. Finally, the ability to hear without hearing is honed to perfection in adulthood. The gentle hum of a pointless homily is much softer on an already deadened ear. That is why Catholics, who pray the penitential prayer of the Church with such devotion, can say the words, *"Ever Virgin,"* and still not believe in them.

Ask the regular churchgoer, "Did the Ever Virgin Mary have other children after the birth of Jesus?"

"Well, I guess she could have," will often enough be the answer.

Then what, may I ask, do the words *Ever Virgin* mean? They seem to resonate with the same passion as a temporary vow of chastity—what's the point?

The Catholic Church does not usually define a dogma, unless someone denies it. There has simply never been a serious threat to this belief about Mary. For a time, a debate did center on the precise nature of her virginity before, during, and after the birth of her only child.

In 649 a Roman synod went so far as to anathematize anyone who denied that Mary was Ever Virgin. However, the Church never got around to making Mary's perpetual virginity a solemnly defined dogma of faith.

At the present time, everyone who believes in Jesus as the only begotten Son of God accepts the virginity of Mary, prior to the conception of Jesus. Today, no one much cares what the words *during the birth* mean with reference to the virginity of Mary. However, the concept of Mary as a virgin, forever after the birth of her

Son, is sometimes debated, although usually only after a few drinks in a poorly lit pub. The virginity of Mary can not be proven, in a scientific way, from Sacred Scripture. There are hints and implications of it, but a critical analysis of those things said about Mary in the bible, lack the precision to establish her virginity with absolute certainty. Nevertheless, there is such a universal agreement concerning her perpetual virginity by almost all of the Greek, Latin, and Syriac Fathers of the Church that its denial is only possible if a substantial part of the Tradition of the Church is rejected. Only Tertullian and Helvidius ever bothered to doubt her virginity after the birth of Jesus.

Tertullian was not only a Father of the Church. He was the Father of Latin theology. His efforts gave a legal stamp to western thought, which still dominates Catholic and Protestant approaches to religion. He invented many of the ways that we speak about God.

However, Tertullian had nothing good to say about anything female. He did write a polemical letter to his wife praising Christian marriage. Tertullian was always eager to use any weapon at his disposal in an argument. One wonders whether he really thought much of marriage, or he just thought so little of anything pagan. If it took praising Christian marriage to beat down pagan marriage, Tertullian was not above swallowing his pride to say something nice about the Christian alternative.

He discouraged marriage, believing that virginity was better. He also discouraged remarriage after the death of a spouse, and then later completely condemned remarriage altogether. He hated women in general and intelligent women in particular. For him, all women were a gate to hell. Those women who presumed to teach anything about God were compared to the desert snakes that lacked any water, notably the water of baptism.

It is not surprising that he made little of the role of Mary in the economy of salvation. None of the great Marian doctrines had been clearly proposed by the time of his death. He did not believe in the perpetual virginity of Mary. It is doubtful that any of the other sublime things that the Church would eventually say about her would have ever occurred to him.

He died some time early in the third century. He wandered away from the Church and went off to pout and die on a lonely sand dune, somewhere in North Africa. The Church was just never harsh enough for his tastes.

Well, he was a brother priest and a creative thinker. Latin Christianity owes him a great debt. Nevertheless, reflecting upon his departure from the Catholic Church, and the final temper tantrum that preceded his solitary death, I can only thank God for leading him into the desert before he had time to get us all into hair shirts. Which I am certain he would have invented, had he lived a little longer.

Tertullian was the only significant early Church Father to doubt the perpetual virginity of the mother of Jesus. The issue would not even surface for any further serious dialogue in the Church until the fourth century.

One of the great constants in the Church is that everyone, and I mean everyone, has an agenda. Sometimes it is expressed. At other times, it is implied. Success in the Church is often a matter of guessing the correct nature of the hidden agenda, and acting accordingly.

Helvidius had such an agenda. He opposed both monasticism and vowed virginity as a way of life. For him, celibate priests were competitors, mostly monks, who threatened his upward career mobility. He wanted to establish a moral equality between marriage and celibacy. He maintained that marriage was in no way inferior to vowed virginity. In fact, he went so far as to claim that Mary had lost her virginity after the birth of Jesus, and bore Joseph other children. Helvidius pointed to the gospel passages that mentioned the *brothers and sisters* of the Lord to proof text his argument.

In his scheme of things, Mary was a neutral figure in the debate over the relative merit of marriage and celibacy. As far as he was concerned, she was the model of both. She had been a virgin at the time of the conception of Jesus. This protected Jesus' status as the only begotten Son of God. However, after the birth of Jesus, she set up housekeeping with Joseph and bore him children in the natural way. He implied that since Mary had been both a virgin mother and later the mother of other children fathered by Joseph, the two ways of living were of equal moral value.

St. Jerome, who had a great deal more in common with Tertullian than history is comfortable admitting, responded to Helvidius.

As a recognized expert in Scripture during the patristic era, Jerome first explained that the brothers and sisters of Jesus mentioned in the gospels were actually his cousins. Jerome maintained that there had not been a word for cousin at the time of the writing of the gospels. He was, of course, incorrect on this point. There did exist a Greek word for cousin, at the time of the writing of the gospels. There was also an Aramaic word, expressing the same relationship. However, he was correct, in as much as there had not been an archaic term for cousin at the time of the redaction of most of the Hebrew Scriptures. It is highly likely that this archaic language of the Jewish Scriptures was used in writing the Christian New Testament. This reflected a reverence for the Hebrew Scriptures, which continued to be reverenced by early Christians.

It's a lot like going to a football game in Kansas City and seeing a banner in the crowd proudly proclaiming, "Yeah, God so loved the world that he gaveth His only begotten Son, that whosoever believeth..." you've got the point. One generation can use the venerable language of the past for added solemnity.

The use of *brother and sister* for what might otherwise have been rendered *cousin* has its contemporary parallels. In any event, Jerome abandoned the idea that there was no Greek or Aramaic word for cousin, and postulated a more acceptable explanation.

There was a somewhat constant tradition, reflected in the *Protoevangelium* of James, that Joseph was quite a bit older than Mary, at the time of the nativity. As an old man, it is highly probable that he had natural married brothers, who had proceeded him in death. According to Jewish law, Joseph would have been obligated to take his brothers' wives and children into his home. He would have been expected to care for his nieces and nephews, as if they were his own children. Thus, Jesus would have grown up in a home filled with children, who would have been recognized as his brothers and sisters, although His mother, Mary, was not their natural mother.

It is significant that, after Helvidius, no other challenge was ever made to the perpetual virginity of Mary. There is near uniformity of agreement on this point among all of the Fathers of the

Church, the scholastics, and even the Protestant reformers. Calvin, Luther, and Zwingli believed Mary to have been Ever Virgin. The largest Protestant church in the world, the Church of the Virgin Mother, sometimes called the *Protestant St. Peter's,* now being renovated in the former East Germany, is a testimony to the Protestant reverence for Mary's virginity. One would do well not to even question Mary's perpetual virginity in the presence of an Orthodox Christian.

The only serious challenge to the consistent belief that Mary is Ever Virgin came sixteen centuries after the death of Helvidius. The first edition of the Dutch Catechism was ambiguous on this point. Its second edition was entirely in line with Sacred Tradition.

Always eager to reinvent the wheel, those seeking a reworked Gnostic form of salvation claim to have discovered an error in Catholic dogma that opens the way for other errors, which might make a more creative sex life easier to rationalize. With clerical celibacy held in general contempt by a great many even within the Church, Mary's perpetual virginity is somewhat of an embarrassment. After all, we are *only* talking about sex. That should have no *real* importance. With the disposal of Mary's continued virginity, any supposed value in living a continent life loses one of its most visible paradigms.

The old argument of Helvidius that marriage and vowed celibacy are of equal value is making a return. The only problem is that this argument made no sense in the fourth century, and it makes none at the beginning of the third millenium.

Unless one maintains that there is no place for asceticism in the Church—a difficult position for anyone who values salvation earned at the cost of a voluntary crucifixion—the denial of any human appetite as a personal gift to God has to mean something.

Unless feasting and fasting are moral equivalents—a position held by an obscure, fourth century, renegade monk named Jovinian—celibacy and marriage can not be moral equivalents. It is true that fasting is easier than feasting, if the food is terrible. It is equally true that some married people experience moments of great difficulty in their lives. After all, nearly half of all married people will experience the death of the person they love the most in life. Many will suffer the illness and loss of children. Some will know the pain of divorce and betrayal. Nevertheless, most married people would agree that celibacy is one blessing seldom desired by those who have been led to marriage.

Personally, I am not ready to make any grand claim that celibacy is a higher calling than marriage. It is simply a different one, and one that has great value for the lived witness of the Church. In general, though not at every moment, it is more difficult than married life. It is the ultimate and permanent cold shower.

If there is no resurrection from the dead, then celibacy makes no sense. In fact, giving up anything that is good in itself makes no sense if this life is all there is. However, if there is a resurrection from the dead and an eternal life that follows, self-denial hints at that life to come. Celibacy then becomes a witness to the reality of eternity.

The Church sometimes preaches with words, but more effectively by concrete lived experience. Celibacy is one of its most profound sermons. It is lived by Latin priests, Eastern bishops, and monks and nuns of both traditions. It is linked to that self-denial that led Jesus to the cross to accomplish our salvation by laying down His life. It is a state of life consecrated and shared by Mary. Her ancient pious titles, prayers dedicated to her, and fragments of early liturgies attest to the constant and original belief that she was *Ever Virgin*.

This, more than any other doctrine of faith, is an example of a dogma proclaimed by the census of the faithful. It rests upon the belief that the Holy Spirit, dwelling within the Church, could not allow the entire Church, everywhere and always, to believe something that was not true. While the institutional Church has never officially proclaimed this teaching, it is certainly a prime candidate for such a dogmatic definition. In announcing what we as the Church already believe, the pope or a Church Council might, one day, decide to tell the world that the Catholic people in it have always believed in Mary's perpetual virginity. At the present time, the perpetual virginity of Mary is an undefined article of faith, so consistently taught by the magisterium of the Church that to deny it places one outside of the community of believers.

Mary is *Ever Virgin*. This is true, not because it is convenient. Its primary importance is that it expresses who Jesus is, as the only begotten Son of the Father. Jesus is not a humanly conceived son, who was later adopted by the Father as His divine Son. That would be Arianism. That would mean that Jesus was no more or less a son of the Father than any baptized Christian. It would also mean that his redemptive death on the cross was of questionable universal effect.

Proclaiming Mary to be the virgin mother of God's only begotten Son is a shorthand way of proclaiming her Son's true identity. Going further and proclaiming her perpetual virginity is about her role as the virginal mother of all believers throughout the rest of human history.

The doctrine of Mary's perpetual virginity is true simply because the Church has always believed it to be true. It is part of that deposit of faith that has been passed down to all generations. It is certainly hinted at in Sacred Scripture. It may have some significance in a discussion of the continued value of vowed sexual continence. However, its real value is in its truth. It tells us who the Father of Jesus is, and, therefore, who Jesus is. It tells us something about Mary and who she is in our lives. Accordingly, she was in the upper room when we were born as Church. We are the spiritual children of a virgin mother.

Mother of God

The Council Fathers gathered in hushed reverence. Each was arrayed in his most impressive vestments. The leader of the assembly rose and with trembling voice solemnly proclaimed Mary to be the *Theotokos*, Mother of God. Every Council Father assented by offering an emotional, *Amen.* Many wept. Some later claimed that they had heard the angels sing a *Gloria.* Outside, the crowd stood in absolute silence. Upon hearing the decision of the Council, many in the crowd dropped to their knees and began to pray in gratitude to God.

Well, so much for the ideal. The truth is that the Council of Ephesus had more in common with a really lusty bar fight, with Texas rules—as everyone knows Texas rules permit eye gouging, ear biting, and any other acts of violence short of actual murder— than a thoughtful deliberation on a title of Mary.

The second thing that all Catholics are challenged to believe concerning Mary is that she is the *Mother of God.* The Perpetual Virginity of Mary is a matter of the census of the faithful. Mother of God is a title, solemnly defined by the Third Ecumenical Council of the Church. Violence, bribery, and public riots were the rules of order for the Third Ecumenical Council.

Background

The wealthy city of Alexandria, Egypt was the home of a school of theology, which stressed the absolute unity of the two natures in Christ. Whatever happened to one nature, happened to the other and, therefore, to the person of Jesus Christ.

Antioch had an equally venerable school of theology. In Antioch, the distinction between the two natures of Christ was stressed. The human nature of Jesus was said to experience things that were not experienced by His divine nature. Thus, for the Antiocheans, Jesus' human nature was born of Mary, but not His divine nature. They taught that Jesus' human nature could suffer, die, and be buried. His divine nature could not.

In 428, a monk from Antioch, Nestorius, was appointed patriarch of Constantinople. The Church of Alexandria had lobbied for one of its candidates to become the patriarch of the capital city and had lost. A bitter taste was left in the collective Alexandrian mouth.

Nestorius was undiplomatic, direct, and perhaps a bit mean. Upon his arrival in Constantinople, he immediately began to deal with heretical elements in the city. It must be remembered that Christianity had only been free from persecution for slightly more than a century. Many of its doctrines had not yet been defined. Theological speculation was a game everyone played. Theology was a hot topic. It was the passionate interest and favorite pastime of nearly everyone. In such an environment, speculation necessarily included probing the boundaries of the faith.

Nestorius was completely unprepared for the task of leading the diverse and theologically active Church of Constantinople. Among his first acts was to preach an impassioned sermon against heresy. Very early in his episcopacy, he sent a letter to Pope Clement I in Rome, in which he described the task before him as one of combating false doctrines. He also explained his difficulty with a title of Mary that had been in common use for at least one hundred years, Theotokos.

In an incredible diplomatic blunder, Nestorius composed his letter in Greek. For several months no one in Rome could read it. The pope was immediately suspect.

Nestorius became increasingly isolated. His heavy handedness made him unpopular with the monks, clergy, and people. His enemies bided their time, waiting for their bishop to make a fatal blunder. He soon gave them their opportunity.

One of the most popular preachers at Constantinople, Proclus, preached a homily in the presence of Nestorius, defending the use of Theotokos. Nestorius took the bait. He now openly attacked the venerable Marian title, ordering his clergy to replace it with Christotokos. In keeping with his Antiochean roots, he maintained that Mary had not given birth to God. She had given birth to the human nature of Christ. Therefore, she should be called *Mother of Christ,* Christotokos.

The people rioted, the monks rebelled, and Alexandria was invited to enter into the controversy. The patriarch of Alexandria was one of the most skillful politicians in the early Church. Cyril immediately saw an opportunity to discredit the traditional rival, Antioch, and improve the influence of Alexandria in both Rome and Constantinople.

He convened a synod in Alexandria to condemn Nestorius' attack upon the Virgin. He then wrote his own letter to Pope Celestine I, setting forth his position. Aware of the shocking decline of scholarship in the West, his letter was tactfully delivered in Latin and well received.

In 430, a Roman Synod adopted Cyril's position. Nestorius appealed to the emperor requesting him to call an Ecumenical Council of the Church.

The emperor, Theodosius I, was perhaps the only individual in the eastern part of the Roman empire who was not interested in the theological consequences of calling Mary Theotokos. He simply wanted peace restored to his empire. All of the great cities of the East were on fire. Riot and bloodshed accompanied the spirited debate over what to call Mary.

Theodosius took Nestorius' suggestion and ordered an Ecumenical Council to assemble at Ephesus on the Feast of Pentecost in 431. Ephesus was chosen because it had become a center of Marian devotion. The great Church at Ephesus had replaced the Temple of Diana. The riot of the silversmiths, recorded in the Acts of the Apostles, would become small potatoes, compared to the months of public unrest which would accompany the Council.

By Easter, Nestorius was already in Ephesus. He gathered a few influential bishops around him and rather naively prepared for the coming conflict. The bishop of Ephesus, Memnon, was not one of Nestorius' supporters. He belonged to the party headed by Cyril of Alexandria. Memnon refused to allow Nestorius to preach in any of the churches of his diocese.

Upon his arrival, Cyril was given free access to those churches, and made use of his prerogative by constantly working the people up to an anti-Nestorian frenzy.

John of Antioch and the Syrian bishops chose the overland rout to Ephesus. Unfortunately, they found themselves traveling through a land experiencing famine and were unable to reach the city by Pentecost.

Pope Celestine's three papal legates had also not yet arrived. Nevertheless, the evening before Pentecost, Cyril announced that the Council would begin the following morning, June 7, 431. Sixty-eight bishops and the imperial representative protested the opening of the Council without the presence of all of the invited bishops.

The imperial representative was listened to by the assembled Council Fathers and then politely invited to depart from the assembly. Nestorius and a few of his supporters refused to attend the Council, which only facilitated his condemnation. One hundred and fifty bishops attended the first session of the Council of Ephesus.

The two letters sent by Cyril to Nestorius were read and adopted as orthodox expressions of the faith of Nicea by the Council. The letter of Nestorius was met with hoots and catcalls. Nestorius was condemned and deposed. The cheers, shouts, and applause of the Council Fathers could be heard by the enormous mob, gathered around the Church of St. Mary.

When, on June 22, the Council decided that Theotokos did, in fact, express the faith of the Church concerning the Person of Jesus and the role of His mother, a wild celebration began. Most of the people of Ephesus made their living in a direct or indirect way from the Marian tourist trade. A more elevated title for Mary was cash in hand for most of the local residents.

The Council Fathers were escorted from the church by a wild throng carrying torches and swinging incense. There were to be five more sessions of the Council. No official notes or records have survived from any of the deliberations. Cyril did record his accounts of the proceedings. However, no official notes or reports from the opposition have survived. In any event, everything of permanent value was accomplished in that first session.

On June 26, John of Antioch and the Syrian bishops reached Ephesus. They gathered outside of the town with Nestorius and the imperial representative, Candidianus. They immediately excommunicated Cyril, along with his supporters. Cyril reciprocated by excommunicating John and the Syrians. Three days later, a letter arrived from Theodosius expressing his extreme disappointment over the entire affair. His only definition of success had been the restoration of peace and unity throughout his empire. In the opinion of the emperor, the Council had been a total failure.

On July 10, the three papal representatives finally arrived from Rome. They called a second session of the Council. The excommunication of Nestorius was ratified. At which time, John of Antioch and the Syrians again withdrew and were, once again, excommunicated, this time for leaving the Council. The Council plodded on until August. By then the emperor had reached the limit of his patience and hope for the Council. Nestorius, Cyril, and Memnon were all deposed and placed under arrest. The rest of the Council Fathers were forced to remain in Ephesus, enjoying the stifling heat of an unbearably hot summer.

Blaming Nestorius for all of the chaos, Theodosius allowed the Council to end and sent home all of the bishops. Cyril and Memnon were restored to their sees. However, the emperor did not recognize the excommunications of John and the Syrians. They also returned to their cities and resumed their ministry. Nestorius was sent to a monastery near Antioch and later was removed to Egypt for closer supervision. He ended his life in obscure irrelevance.

This was not quite the end of the story. Cyril recognized that the theological debate would only be finally settled if the secular power of the state enforced the decisions of the Council. He used the incredible wealth of Alexandria to win favor with those individuals who were powerful at the imperial court. His lavish gifts included ivory chairs, ostriches, and gold—more than one million dollars worth of incentives by contemporary standards. He also called upon the monks of the capital city for support.

Theodosius got the message. His imperial government and the powerful monasteries in and near Constantinople seemed to have a growing passion for the title, defined at Ephesus.

Eventually, Cyril and John brokered a deal bringing peace to the empire and a complete acceptance of Theotokos.

Actually, the title, *Mother of God*, was never about Mary. It was about the two natures of Jesus Christ and his Personhood. Was Jesus a kind of human puppet, with a God hand inside moving Him around? Or was Jesus Christ a true person, who really was born, really hurt, and really died? If only the human part of Him died on the cross, it was difficult to see how that mere human death was great enough to atone for every inhuman act mankind would ever commit for as long as human history continued. If, on the other hand, God could hang on the cross and die, was the omnipotence and majesty of God protected?

The Council Fathers opted for the unity of the two natures of the Person, Christ. Whatever happened to the Person happened to both his human and his divine nature. Therefore, since the Person of Jesus was born of Mary, and since that Person had two natures, one human and the other divine, Mary, as the mother of the Person, Jesus, was the mother of God. The title is about her only in a secondary way. It is about Jesus and about how He accomplished our salvation.

Holy Mary, Mother of God, pray for us sinners now and at the hour of our death. Amen

The Immaculate Conception

There are three ways through which a teaching of the Church can be established as dogma. The first is by the census of the faithful. Since the Holy Spirit has been given to the entire Church, anything believed by everyone, everywhere, is always a part of the deposit of faith left to us by Jesus. Therefore, even though the Perpetual Virginity of Mary has never been officially defined, it is taught by the Church and is binding on all believers.

The second way a dogma becomes established is by an act of an Ecumenical Council of the Church. A Council possesses the fullness of apostolic authority. One can no more argue with a Council than one could argue with an apostle. The authority of the Church is one. Therefore, the Council may never declare anything that is opposed to the fundamental Revelation of the Father, Scripture and Tradition. In a sense, it never defines new doctrines, but announces what the Church has always believed. It simply proclaims to the entire world that a particular article of faith is already part of the faith of every believing member of the Church. The Council makes its pronouncements in union with the pope. It is not superior to him. In fact, when a pope dies during a Council, the Council ceases functioning until a new pope calls it back into session.

The third way a dogma can be defined is by an act of the pope when he is speaking on behalf of the entire Church. He is the only bishop who may speak on behalf of all the other bishops, who share the apostolic office. Each of the other bishops speaks only for his own diocese. The pope, alone, speaks for the entire Church.

The pope is not free to declare just anything a dogma of faith. He acts upon his own authority, but is infallible only when he defines something already believed by the Church. He could not, for example, have a bad day and declare ham and eggs to be a sacrament of the Church. He could not define Mary as god or declare that only women go to heaven. The Church does not believe such things and, therefore, the pope could not announce them as part of the faith of the Church. Nevertheless, it is not safe to go on at length concerning what popes can not do. Let's move on.

Two of the ways the Church establishes dogma have already been illustrated by the Marian doctrines, Ever Virgin and Mother of God. The Immaculate Conception is the third article of faith that all Catholics believe about Mary. The solemn proclamation of Mary's Immaculate Conception was also the first instance of a pope defining a dogma on his own authority.

Pope Pius IX defined the doctrine of the Immaculate Conception in 1854, fourteen years before the First Vatican Council got around to proclaiming that a pope could define dogma on his own authority. Nevertheless, by the middle of the nineteenth century, one could see the direction the future Council would go. Pope Pius IX called the Council into session on December 8, 1868, the feast of the Immaculate Conception.

This Council was destined to never finish its work. It defined the pope to be infallible when he spoke *ex cathedra* on faith and morals. Then, it adjourned so that the French and German bishops could return to their warring nations. The Council never reconvened. This left the dogma of papal infallibility unmitigated and unsupported by the real work of the Council, a document on the Church. Without that document, infallibility seemed to float without a sea. It made the pope look like an absolute dictator. Instead of the voice of the Church, he spoke with naked power. Such was not the intention of the Council. It was merely the result of unfinished work. The Second Vatican Council corrected this contextual vacuum by first defining the Church and then identifying roles within the Church.

When the First Vatican Council gathered, the bishops debated the need to ratify the papal pronouncement concerning the Immaculate Conception. In a collateral issue, it considered defining the Assumption as a dogma of faith. The Council Fathers agreed that neither definition was necessary. The pope, who would be declared to be infallible, had already defined the Immaculate Conception, and further definition of the Assumption seemed unnecessary, since the Church already believed it, and no one was making a challenge to it.

Background

The primary difficulty in proclaiming the doctrine of the Immaculate Conception was that some of the most important minds in the Church had difficulty accepting it. Sts. Augustine, Anselm, Bernard, Albert the Great, Bonaventure, Thomas Aquinas, and Alexander of Hales believed that if Mary had been conceived without sin, then the salvation, accomplished by Christ would not apply to her. To avoid any implication of impurity in the Virgin, most of these great thinkers agreed that Mary was conceived with sin, but cleansed from it while still inside the womb. They believed that to exempt Mary entirely from the salvation won by her Son would destroy the universality of Christ's redemption. There would be at least one human being for whom He did not die. At the same time, piety would not allow any suggestion that the Virgin Mother was somehow lacking in the fullness of grace.

Duns Scotus broke the impasse. He explained that Mary needed the redemption won by her Son, more than any other person who ever lived. Christ could not be the perfect Mediator unless he could preserve his own mother from sin, and God could not be perfectly appeased unless at least one human being could be completely preserved from the sin of Adam. That one person was Mary.

Following Scotus' reasoning, the Council of Basil declared the Immaculate Conception to be a dogma of the faith. Unfortunately, this Council had broken with the pope and was not, therefore, a Council of the Church. Its doctrines were not binding.

Between 1627 and 1644 the Roman inquisition decreed that the term *Immaculate Conception* could not be used. Instead one had to speak of the conception of the immaculate Virgin.

In 1708 the Immaculate Conception became a universal feast of the Church. The apparition of Mary to St. Catherine Laboure in 1830, and the subsequent devotion to the *Miraculous Medal* provided the Immaculate Conception with a popular universal following. Momentum for the dogmatic definition of the Immaculate Conception was growing.

The Church in the United States made an important contribution to the establishment of the dogma of the Immaculate Conception. In 1843, the sixth provincial council of Baltimore petitioned the pope to declare the Immaculate Conception, patroness of the United States. Pius IX did so, the following year.

Cardinal Newman believed the Immaculate Conception to be a doctrine flowing from the *New Eve* image of Mary. He considered it to be part of the Tradition handed down by the apostles.

In defining the Immaculate Conception, Pius IX appealed to his brother bishops throughout the world. The early years of Pius IX pontificate were marked by his openness. His later years seemed less so. In 1858, he announced that practically all of the responding bishops wished him to define the Immaculate Conception as an article of faith. He acceded to their requests on December 8, 1854, in the Apostolic Constitution, *Ineffabilis Deus.*

We declare, pronounce, and define that the doctrine which holds that the most Blessed Virgin Mary, in the first instant of her Conception, by a singular grace and privilege granted by Almighty God, in view of the merits of Jesus Christ, the Savior of the human race, was preserved free from all stain of original sin, is a doctrine revealed by God and therefore to be believed firmly and constantly by all the faithful.

This dogma had a long and colorful history. It was more philosophical than most statements issued by the Church. It did not only speak of the soul of Mary. In fact, by insisting on her sinlessness from the first moment of her human conception, it linked the condition of her soul to that of her body.

I have stressed the difficulties experienced by many of the most important minds of the Church in accepting the Immaculate Conception to emphasise the nature of the lively debate that has accompanied this doctrine. There were, of course, many early Fathers of the Church who upheld Mary's absolute sinlessness from the first moment of her conception. That has always been the recognized significance of the angel's greeting to her, "Full of Grace." Where there is the fullness of grace, sin can not abide. Certainly, no Christian would ever attack the purity of the Virgin.

The difficulties with this doctrine had little to do with her. They were about her Son, and the universality of his redemption. Once again, the significance of the concept was Christological. Was Christ the Savior of the entire human race, or not? Was Mary the only person who ever lived not needing His redemption? In defining the Immaculate Conception, the pope made it abundantly clear that Mary not only needed redemption by her Son, she needed it more than any human being who ever lived. The old Eve was the original sinner. The new Eve was as free from sin as the original Eve before the fall, but only because her Son's perfect act of redemption anticipated her unique vocation to be the Mother of Salvation.

The Assumption

Between 1849 and 1950, numerous petitions requesting that the Assumption of the Blessed Virgin Mary into heaven be defined as a dogma reached Rome. One hundred and thirteen cardinals, eighteen patriarchs, two thousand-five hundred and five bishops, more than fifty thousand religious women, and eight million lay people had requested this definition. The increase in worldwide Marian devotion had grown so extensive that Pope Puis XII determined, early in his pontificate, that he would consider declaring Mary to be Assumed, body and soul, into heaven.

In 1946, the pope began a process leading to his solemn declaration of the Assumption of Mary. In imitation of Pius IX, he sent an encyclical letter, *Deiparae Virginis,* to the bishops of the world, asking their opinion of the Assumption. Only twenty-two of the one thousand-one hundred and eighty-one responding bishops had reservations in proclaiming the dogma. Of these twenty-two dissenting bishops, only six doubted that the Assumption could be defined as a doctrine of faith. The remainder simply believed that it was not opportune to define the Assumption at that time.

Pius XII abandoned the route of establishing a historical link between contemporary belief in the Assumption and that of the church of the apostles. Nor did he attempt to prove it using scripture. Instead he appealed to the lived faith of the Church. The uniformity of the responding bishops, who spoke for the people in their dioceses, was to be the foundation of this dogma.

The pope used the already established feast of the Assumption, the numerous churches, cities and towns named for it, and the popular devotion of the people, who invoked the Assumption in the recitation of the rosary, as indications that this mystery was already part of the faith of the Church. On November 1, 1950, Pius XII defined the Assumption of Our Lady as a dogma of faith in the Apostolic Constitution, *Munificentissimus Deus.*

He avoided the question of Mary's death. This had been a thorny problem in days when the story of the fall of Adam and Eve was considered to be a strict, literal, historical account. Since sin and death entered into the world through the first Eve, could the second, sinless Eve experience one of the primary effects of original sin, death?

The question may seem unimportant at the present time. Nevertheless, this had been a hot topic of debate in the Church for several centuries. No one paid much attention to the fact that Jesus, who died on the cross, was also without original sin. In any event, Pius XII chose to avoid this topic. The three empty tombs of Mary in Jerusalem, one Franciscan, one Benedictine and one Orthodox continue to be rival places, described by the ambiguous term, *the place of Mary's falling asleep.* Whether she died or just rested until she was taken into heaven, the Church has solemnly declared that she was the first member of the Church to experience what all of the faithful members of the Church will one day experience.

This dogma is also about Jesus. He came to earth to give the human race a new start, a second chance. Unless at least one human being has escaped the curse of Adam and Eve, He had failed. Mary was that single example of the defeat and total destruction of the effects of original sin.

Where she has gone we shall be taken, not by our own efforts, but as the result of the free gift of grace, given to us by the new Adam. Jesus not only destroyed the power of sin; He also completed what the Father had begun in Paradise.

He continues to lead us toward that purpose, for which we were all created. He will, one day, take us body and soul into heaven. The story will then be complete. What has happened to Mary will happen to us, because of who her Son was and because of what He has accomplished.

In the final analysis, everything the Church says concerning Mary is about who Jesus was, and what His life, death, and resurrection means to the entire human race. It is difficult to imagine exaggerating our gratitude to her. She was only a door through which our Salvation passed, but without that door where would we be?

BONE 4

Immigration

Strangers and Aliens
No Longer

While I have attempted to relate only the truth as I know it, I thought it prudent to change the names of the individuals described in this chapter.

We call the Church *Catholic* because it is supposed to be universal. By its name, we proclaim it to be the Church that belongs to every age, every place, every culture, and every people. We say that in our creed.

In the early days of our republic, it was not at all clear that Catholics were equal members of the political community. As immigration increased and this nation became more Catholic, many of the anti-immigrant feelings that were incited by the *Know-nothings* and the *Klan* were directed toward Irish, Italian, German, and Polish immigrants precisely because they were also Catholic. The claim that the Democratic Party was the party of *rum, rebellion, and Rome* was hardly a compliment.

We were the outsiders. We were the poor. We were thought of as the non-English speaking. We were the job takers, the scabs and the foreigners. It took several generations and our own school system to move us from the poorest white members of society, to the best educated and the wealthiest members of the community. We, the great-grandchildren of those hated immigrants, are now Americans in every way.

At the present time, a new wave of immigration has swept into the land. Once again, the newcomers are mostly Catholic. Like most of those immigrants who came to this land in the past, their native language is not English. They are poor, often lacking in formal education, and willing to work for wages that most of us would never consider. Part of the unfortunate truth is that many of the grandchildren of hated immigrants now do the hating.

Our nation has never been more prosperous. Unemployment is so low that many parts of the country are experiencing a serious shortage of entry level, unskilled workers. There has never been a time when it would have been easier to absorb new people into our country. Yet, we fear the Asian and Hispanic immigrants coming to America.

We seem to be afraid that they will take our jobs, move into our neighborhoods, flood our welfare system, destroy the character of our schools, and make our nation less white and less English speaking. Some might even fear that our nation may become less Protestant. Although, that seems unlikely, since the Catholic Church does such a poor job keeping the new arrivals Catholic.

I have always been something of a patriot. I enlisted in the marines after college, and later accepted a commission as an officer. I requested to be sent to Vietnam. I have never failed to vote in any national election, and I believe in defending my nation's borders.

I remember reading a story about the southern border of our nation. It reported that our border with Mexico was almost completely open. That angered me. I even considered writing a letter to the editor of the local newspaper, demanding that our country keep out the unwanted law-breakers, who were attempting to come into America illegally. God has never failed to knock me down, when I get that high on a horse.

I was preparing to celebrate the early mass at St. Joseph of Apple Creek. I had been given the most beautiful parish in the Archdiocese of St. Louis. I lived very well, and was hardly overworked. I had time to tend the garden, pray and read. All of that was about to come to a rather abrupt end.

I got the call at approximately 7:30 a.m. It was the Archbishop, asking me to become the pastor of St. Francis de Sales parish. When I responded with an immediate, "Yes," the Archbishop seemed a little surprised.

I knew very little about my new parish. It had a magnificent church, nicknamed *The Cathedral of South St. Louis*. While I could never find it in print, people boasted that it had the tallest church tower in the mid-west. De Sales had been one of the great parishes. However, in recent years it had suffered blight, flight, and neglect. The parish plant was in need of several million dollars worth of repairs. Everything needed immediate attention. The magnificent stained glass was in danger of falling out. The floor was buckling, the plaster was flaking off, and the church tower was pulling away from the rest of the building.

Its two enormous boilers provided sporadic heat, with vintage 1930 efficiency. The rectory had several rooms with collapsing ceilings. They were closed off. One room had several buckets of stagnant water, from the rain that came through the ceiling. Dead rats and mice lay decaying on the carpet, near bits of poison bait.

In spite of its shocking state of disrepair, the rectory was in better shape than most of the other parish buildings. The upper floors of the old school building had been unoccupied for several decades. Empty buildings just seem to decay, as soon as they become empty. This one was on its way to irreversible blight.

The former convent was half renovated. Tens of thousands of dollars would be needed to finish that job. The adjoining *new* school—forty years old—was empty. The consolidated grade school, of the five contiguous parishes, had moved to another parish, leaving our abandoned building to deteriorate.

The parish debt had grown by fifty thousand dollars, each of the past five years, to an impossible quarter of a million dollars. Only about three hundred souls attended the three Sunday masses offered in English. The main mass accommodated the majority of these people. To look out over a congregation of no more than two hundred, in a church that seated over one thousand, was like presiding over a sinking ship. The other two English masses, each with less than fifty worshipers, were difficult to justify.

Not everyone who attended these masses could speak English. A small number of Vietnamese, Laotians, Cambodians, and Africans worshiped with the English-speaking members of the parish. About three hundred Spanish-speaking people attended mass in their native language. Their numbers were about to increase, dramatically.

Counting the Hispanic members of the parish was an art, more than a science. Many of our Hispanic people were in the country illegally. They were suspicious of leaving any kind of paper trail. The city had passed an ordinance mandating residency within the city limits by all municipal employees. Threats had been made to use church records to prove or disprove residency for police officers and firemen. The lesson was not lost on our Spanish-speaking parishioners. Registration drives, targeting the Hispanics, never identified more than a tiny handful of the people who regularly worshipped in our church.

Even the word *regular* did not really apply to most Hispanic members of the parish. The concept of mandatory Sunday mass attendance meant little to people for whom the availability of mass every Sunday was an unexpected luxury. Back home, most of our Latino brothers and sisters had simply gathered in the local church for mass, whenever a priest came to town. That might mean mass once each month or twice each year, but attending mass every Sunday had not been possible for most of them.

Local conditions of employment also gravitated against weekly mass attendance. Some of the people before me worked seven days every week for illegal wages, far below the minimum wage. If they came late and left early, they were probably on their way to work. Some could attend mass only once each month, on a rare day off. Still others took an occasional Sunday off from mass, to spend time in the park with their family. I could not advocate that, but I certainly could understand it. Sunday mass in Spanish was always at noon. By that time, all the nice places in the park had been taken. Was a family never to enjoy a day in the park, the one pleasure that reminded them of home?

Other ways of counting noses were equally illusive. Not one of the nationalities within the Hispanic community had ever experienced a Sunday envelope. Some came from countries in which the government closely controlled the Church's ability to collect funds. For the rest, a lifetime of dropping a few precious pesos into the collection basket was not going to be overcome in a few weeks or months. It is true that past immigrants built some of the most impres sive Catholic buildings presently gracing many of our great cities. They did this in their poverty often going without basic necessities to build the Church in America. However, they also received a welcome from the Church that made its survival possible. They were sometimes given loans to buy homes or land, at nominal interest rates. They were sometimes fed, clothed, and transported to areas of the country where they could begin a decent life. Yes, it is true that some new immigrants find it difficult to contribute to the local Church. But it is also true that the local Church seems to lack its past zeal in welcoming the new immigrants.

Another major difference between the old immigrants and the new is that the old waves of immigration included members of the clergy. Today, most Spanish-speaking immigrants come from Mexico. In the middle part of the twentieth century an anti-clerical revolution destroyed many of the basic institutions of the Catholic Church. Seminaries and other Catholic educational institutions were either destroyed or confiscated. In some places, priests were hunted down and murdered. Until very recently, a young man who became a priest lost his Mexican citizenship and had to carry a Vatican passport in his own country. Mexico simply does not have the priests to send with its migrating people.

Even if it did, American Church politics would work against the Mexican clergy coming to the States in imitation of earlier Irish, German, and Italian priests. The Universal Church displays no eagerness to augment the American shortage of clergy by emptying Third World countries of their native priests. There are also fearful elements of the American Church that see an imported priesthood as a means of delaying their agenda for the American Church. It is sometimes whispered that the foreign priests who come to America bring a conservative ecclesiology with them that interferes with the *direction* of the American Church.

Therefore, the new immigrants are often either left unserved or served by those American priests who speak Spanish. Even the most fluent Spanish-speaking American priest knows little of the cultural assumptions shared by many of those Catholics who come to this country from Hispanic countries.

At the same time, the old welcome that the Catholic Church extended to past immigrants is being extended to the newcomers. However, Protestant congregations more often extend it these days. The drain of Latino Catholics into Protestant denominations is obvious. What is not so obvious is the cultural destruction of life back in priestless villages all over the Latin American world.

Apostates from the Catholic faith often return home. They bring with them an alien faith and an alien way of life, but many times they also bring with them needed medicine, food, and clothing. Those things are usually accompanied by challenges of *why isn't your Church doing something for you?*

Over night, the fabric of ancient cultures is ripped in two. Town festivals, public prayers, and rhythms of life that have provided social identities for half a millenium are held in bitter contempt by some of the returning expatriates. Local Catholics often counter them with signs posted to their doors saying *"This is a Catholic Home; We Accept No Protestant Propaganda."* Those signs are about as effective as they would be in our own country.

Many of the new Hispanic immigrants who worshiped with us at St. Francis de Sales lived outside of the physical boundaries, of the parish. They were drawn by the use of their native language and a familiar liturgy. For a little more than one hour each week, they were not foreigners or outsiders. They were just Catholic people at mass.

Each of the twenty-eight Spanish-speaking nationalities had its own set of customs and expectations. However, the largest part of our Hispanic people came from Mexico. Other than their Catholic faith, about the only constant shared by all of them was that they were under assault by proselytizing groups. Flyers with color pictures of Our Lady of Guadeloupe were often left under their windshield wipers while they attended mass. The flyers promised a free Catholic bible to anyone who called the phone number on the pamphlet. A Spanish-speaking evangelist usually delivered the bible. This would often be the first of many visits, welcome or unwelcome. During every one, he would challenge the Catholic faith of the family whose only concern had been acquiring a free, Spanish language, Catholic bible.

On more than one occasion, such flyers had been handed in Church, during mass. Coupled with the offer of free medical care and free contraception, this strategy was sometimes effective.

On big feasts—Palm Sunday, Good Friday and Our Lady of Guadeloupe—the Church was nearly full. It was also full, to standing room only, on First Communion day. My estimate of the number of Spanish-speaking Catholics who called the parish their own, was somewhere near three thousand. That does not mean that three thousand attended Sunday mass every week. However, it meant that if the Hispanics were counted in the same way that the other Catholic members of the parish were counted, including the inactive and Christmas Catholics, that our parish had grown to include several thousand Hispanic and three hundred English-speaking Catholics. However, only a few hundred of those who spoke Spanish attended mass every Sunday.

Since I could not speak a word of Spanish, my immediate concern was to establish some means of communicating with those people I had been given to love who could not speak my language.

The parish council had only recently voted to allow the Hispanic members of the community to register as parishioners. I admit that I was completely taken back by this. My understanding of Church was that every baptized Catholic who came to our parish church was already a member of the parish, and needed no one's permission to take full part in the active life of the parish.

However, at de Sales everything had a history. I was informed that the Hispanics had rented the Church, for twelve previous years. They paid for the privilege of having one mass in Spanish each week. The decision to allow them to join the parish was seen as a step forward. Nevertheless, it seemed to me that if the parish council had the right to invite a particular ethnic group into the parish, it might just as easily invite one out. Still, I saw no reason to resume past battles, based on theory. Our Hispanic brothers and sisters were now part of the family, and I, as their pastor, had to find a way to minister to all of the people.

Priests who spoke Spanish with varying degrees of fluency, had served the Hispanic community. The brightest star among them was a young Jesuit from Columbia, Padre Jeremio. Even though I did not speak Spanish, I made it a point to concelebrate every Spanish mass. Eventually, I was able to recite a few paragraphs of the Eucharistic Prayer in their language. Padre Jeremio seemed as excited about what we were attempting to do as I was.

Blending peoples of so many cultures and language groups was like being present at the first Pentecost. Our work was beginning to pay off. Within the first year, five young people identified themselves as interested in the priesthood or religious life. By the end of my second year, two young women, Clorita and Louisa, had entered convents. Loupe, Javier, and Oscar began working toward their dream of becoming priests.

Clorita was born in Missouri. Louisa was a Puerto Rican. Both of these women were American citizens. However, not only were the three young men not citizens, none of them was in the country legally.

I had always thought of myself as politically conservative. Now, I was faced with ministering to members of my parish who were breaking the law by their very presence. What was I to do?

I chose to begin ministering to any and all who came to our parish. The alternative would have been to hold up the Eucharist at communion time and say, "The Body of Christ, are you legal?" I decided to place my priesthood ahead of my citizenship.

It is remarkable how quickly points of view change, when people come to know each other. I admit falling in love with the people of my new parish—all of them. I grew especially fond of the three young men who wanted to become priests.

Javier, twenty-one years old, had been in this country since the age of nine. He had been sold to a family, to care for two children with cerebral palsy. He had never been allowed to attend school, and had never learned English. He carried the scars of physical punishment on his back. By the age of eighteen, he was strong enough to fight back. He left the only home he had known since early childhood, and began to make his way in a foreign world. He supported himself by doing odd jobs and landscaping. Like most of our Hispanic people, he would have never considered help from a social service or government agency.

He taught himself to play music, and became a master of the keyboard and guitar. He loved to sing, and did so quite well. He played guitar for the choir, daily growing closer to the Church.

One Sunday, he told a Hispanic lay leader that he dreamed of some day being a priest. That seemed highly unlikely, since he could neither legally attend school nor hold a job.

When I asked him if it was true that he wanted to be a priest, he said, "Yes." I later discovered that if I had asked him if he wanted me to beat him in the head with a shovel, he would have also answered, "Yes." That was the only English word he knew. He would have said nothing else to any priest. I decided to try to help him.

Loupe was an entirely different case. This young man had finished his third year of theology in Mexico. He had an identical twin, Ascension. Both young men had been together since birth. Both wanted priesthood. However, their parents lived in a simple two-room, adobe house. They had more resources than most people did in the village. Nevertheless, keeping both of their sons in the seminary had completely bankrupted the family. Reluctantly, they called their sons home and told them that one would have to leave the seminary. The family was heavily in debt. There was simply not enough money for both of the young men to remain in school. Loupe and Ascension flipped a coin. Loupe lost.

The brothers worked out a plan between them. Loupe would go to the States and find work. He would send back as much money as he could, to pay off the debts of both brothers. Then he would return after his brother's ordination and *Padre* Ascension would pay Loupe's way through the seminary, with his priest's salary. Loupe was arrested the day he crossed the border!

I have dealt with immigration officers many times. I have never known one who was not a good and decent human being. They are patriotic. They do the best they can to enforce the law, and show human compassion to those they apprehend and deport. Often, they had asked me to find temporary guesthouses for women and children who had been arrested and were waiting for deportation. I did not like participating in that process, but I felt that anything that kept children out of jail had to be attempted.

When Loupe was arrested, the holding cells were so full, that he had to be sent to the county jail. Somehow his case became lost, and he remained in jail for the next six months. He was confined in a general population of violent criminals. He could not even speak to these people. His life became a nightmare.

The one time he tried to describe what had happened to him in jail, he broke down and began to cry. He was unable to put into words what he had experienced. I was ashamed for my country.

After six months, Loupe was dumped south of the border. He returned that same day. His brother had to have the money to continue his studies for the priesthood.

This time Loupe made his way to St. Louis. He got a job in a restaurant, earning less than two dollars an hour. That varied because he was paid by the month and not by the hour. He worked twelve-hour days, six days each week, and came in Sunday to clean the kitchen, without pay. He had been working for a year, when he was brought to my attention. I asked him if he still wanted to become a priest. When he said, "Yes," I decided to help him.

Oscar, the youngest of my three Hispanic brothers, was full of life. I never saw him without a smile on his face. He had been in this country for enough years to learn English and get a high school diploma. His family was supportive. Upon hearing that Oscar wanted to test his vocation, his family moved to St. Louis from California. They wanted to be with him, in the adventure of working toward ordination. I decided to help him.

After initial inquiries with the vocation office, I learned that there would be no way for any of the Hispanics to attend the seminary unless they were legal residents, could speak English, and had family members living within the boundaries of the Archdiocese.

There is, at present, no way for a Mexican who is in the country illegally to become a legal resident. The only hope for an undocumented Mexican to become a legal resident is to return to Mexico, and apply for legal reentry into the States. I gathered as many documents as possible, and sent Javier and Loupe back to Mexico. Oscar had a good job, and wanted to work a little longer before testing his vocation.

I had no idea what people went through just to apply for admission into this country. Gathering the legal papers from the Mexican government to apply for permission to leave the country is difficult enough. Getting a visa to enter the United States is nearly impossible.

The U.S. embassy is next door to one of the most luxurious hotels in Mexico City, the Sheraton Maria Isabel. The street between the hotel and embassy is blocked off. It begins filling with people in the early hours of the morning. Most people hoping for a visa sleep on the sidewalk or in the street. Each morning hundreds, sometimes thousands, of people gather. Each has a pathetic hope that he or she will be one of the few lucky individuals to get permission to come to the States. Only a few visas are issued each day. Many of the people who gathered outside of the American embassy are not even allowed to make application. They have none of the skills that we want from new immigrants. Those with professional degrees have a chance of being allowed to immigrate.

Often I hear people say that *those illegals* should get into line, and wait their turn. The truth is that the vast majority of poor people, who are willing to work very hard for a better life, are simply not allowed to get into line. We value only wealthy, highly educated, or unusually talented candidates for immigration.

In my opinion, this devalues our own working people. Are only highly educated people of value? Are the only real Americans, our own college-educated natives? When it comes to allowing people to enter the country, working class people—the kind of people who built this nation—simply have no value.

I waited in the street until Javier and Loupe were allowed into the processing center. Then I went into the hotel for breakfast. Once again, I was horrified. The breakfast buffet was set up on the first floor, street level. After filling my plate from the all-you-can-eat buffet, I seated myself at a table near the window. Inches from my plate were the faces of hungry children, watching my food. These were the children of those who had already entered the processing center. They waited sleepy, cold, and hungry. Their little faces were pressed against the glass of the window. I was unable to eat.

After several hours of processing, Loupe came out of the side door with his visa. Javier's request was denied. During the questioning, he had admitted being in the United States illegally. That was enough to bar him from receiving a visa. I had brought him to

Mexico, and now had to leave him there, without any means of earning a living.

Exactly how I managed to eventually get him a legal visa will remain my little secret. One morning, the U.S. embassy in Mexico City called to tell me that *they* had decided to allow Javier to have a visa. I expressed my gratitude. It had taken nearly a full year to get him back into the country legally. The impossible had happened once again.

Loupe and Javier were now legally in the country, but only on student visas. They could not legally work. Loupe graduated first in his class, in the *English as a Second Language* program, of one of the world's great universities. Javier was able to pass, but only barely. Not bad for a kid who had never before set foot in a classroom.

It was obvious that these young men would still have a difficult time being accepted into the local seminary. There was no program for Hispanic theologians. Nevertheless, through persistence, and the relocation of a married brother to St. Louis, Loupe was eventually accepted. However, it was crystal clear that his credits from the Mexican seminary meant practically nothing. He would be starting over. Javier also started over, in high school. We kept the fact that he was in his twenties to ourselves.

The summer before Loupe's entrance into theology, his brother was ready for ordination to the priesthood. I insisted that Loupe return home for this important event in the lives of both brothers. Loupe protested that the trip home was too expensive. I gave him little choice in the matter. Some life-long regrets can easily be avoided.

Loupe left for his home village, two weeks before the ordination. I joined him, the day before his brother became a priest.

The road into Palmar Grande is not much better than a dry Missouri riverbed. For the last three miles of the trip, my rental car failed to reach five miles per hour.

I have always been afflicted with romanticism. I immediately fell in love with Loupe's village. His home was simple, but very beautiful. Tropical trees shaded the house. His mother, Francesca, seemed to never stop working. She was up before dawn every morning, grinding coffee with a stone, and making fresh tortillas.

The smoke from the wood fire on the porch wafted into the *guestroom*. Every morning that I stayed in that house, I awoke to a wonderful sweet smell. My eyes opened to see stars, through the spaces between the clay tiles above me. There were no mechanical sounds—no cars, air-conditioners, or small motors driving appliances. It is remarkable how many daily noises surround us. We never know that, until we wake up, and hear real quiet, for the first time in years.

Loupe's father, Philippe, seemed at peace with his world. He provided everything that the family needed. He kept the cistern, in front of the house, full of fresh water. Ears of corn hung on a pole, over the cistern. Philippe watched his ten cattle, closely. There were no luxuries. In truth, many of the things I had come to think of as necessities were simply not needed.

The house had two beds, four chairs, a table, and two platforms for cooking food and washing dishes. Four unmatched coffee cups hung on nails.

These good people kept their own schedule. They ate meals at times unfamiliar to me and worked hours that seemed odd. They were the cleanest people that I had ever encountered. None of the men or women who so much as drank a cup of coffee would do so without washing their hands and arms up to the elbow. They were also the most generous people I had ever been among. When the town drunk wandered by the house, and saw the *gringo* guest, he came up, and was seated with the family at table as if he were the most welcomed of honored guests. Although, Francesca did make it clear that his drunken state was less than appropriate.

The village was alive with outsiders. Many people had walked for days to take part in Padre Ascension's first mass. Loupe's father had killed one of his precious cattle to celebrate his son's ordination. The houseguests stayed up late into the night, talking about the significance of having a new priest from the village. Everyone felt a part of what was about to take place. Several people pledged to live better lives, more worthy of having a priest in the family.

The ordination took place the next morning in the cathedral city. The crowd was expected to be so large that the cathedral could not be used. A huge tent was set up in the plaza. The cathedral was used as a vesting place for concelebrating priests.

The crowd began arriving early. It was considerably larger than anyone had expected. If it had not been for the teenagers who locked arms and held back the crowd there would have been no way for the priests to reach the altar. The young people did the best they could to clear a path for the priests and those who were about to be ordained. As the concelebrants pushed their way through the people, rose petals were showered upon them. The five candidates for ordination received wild applause, as did Bishop Carlos.

The mass was a cultural expression of who the people were. The bishop embraced each new priest, and kissed him on the cheek, the way a father kisses his only son. Immediately after being ordained, the young priests came down to their families, and their own parents washed the holy oil from their anointed hands. Then the clergy was called forward to offer a sign of peace to their new priest brothers. Every priest, old and young, reverently kissed the hands of the new priests.

As I approached Padre Ascension, to kiss his hands, Loupe suddenly got a case of the giggles. He knew how uncomfortable I was when Mexicans kissed my hands. Loupe took great satisfaction in watching me kiss his brother's hands. In fact, he fell off his chair laughing.

That night, I sat in a small cinder block room with the five new priests. They immediately began calling each other, "Padre." I thought that odd, since I seldom call my brother priests, "Father," when we are alone. It also seemed strange, since each of the new priests, and all of the seminarians, called the bishop by his first name.

I provided one beer for each of the newly ordained. That was the formal reception. After a few minutes, I noticed that I was the only person in the room wearing shoes. I kicked mine off. After our brief celebration, we left for Palmar Grande.

The next morning, Padre Ascension celebrated his first mass in his hometown. Just as in the cathedral city, the local parish church could not accommodate the crowd. Most of the people in his town had been unable to attend the ordination. They traveled on foot to his first mass.

The morning of the first mass, I was awakened by music outside my window. It was not for me. It was for Padre Ascension.

During the night, the people of his village had covered the road from his parent's house to the town square with flowers. The priests and the bishop walked on a carpet of flowers, to the center of town. The people walked beside us forming a protective honor guard. Everyone sang, "Viva Christo Rey!" over and over, until we arrived at the platform that had been erected in the center of town.

The bishop preached at this, and at each of the other first masses. The people applauded often, and with enthusiasm. Finally, it was Padre Ascension's turn to speak. He thanked his parents, friends, teachers, and his bishop. Then he thanked me. I could only understand a little of what he said, but I made out that he was thanking me for taking care of his brother. Then he fell apart and began to weep, loudly. Loupe buried his face in his hands, and cried along with his brother. The pain of being apart had finally come to the surface. At that moment, I knew that Loupe would not be returning with me, to *North America,* to begin his studies in the seminary.

After the mass, a wonderful party began. Loupe's family had prepared most of the food in large fifty-five gallon metal drums. There were enough beans, rice, and tortillas for everyone. The honored guests got meat, and all the children got a piece of cake—a rare and wonderful treat.

The bishop asked if he could speak to Loupe, in private. They separated themselves from the rest of the crowd, and from me. I could see my young friend nodding his head, yes. When the conversation ended, the bishop got out of town, quickly, and Loupe approached me, like a condemned man.

"Father John, I think that you should have something to drink, now," was the way he began this important conversation.

"No, Loupe, your mescal makes me sick. I'd rather have a coke."

"No, Father John, I think that you will need a drink."

"Why, my friend, because you are about to tell me you are staying in Mexico?"

Loupe said nothing for a moment. Then he began to thank me for all I had done for him. I stopped him in mid-sentence, and told him how proud I was of him, and how happy I was that he would be returning to the seminary in his home diocese.

He seemed overwhelmed. His brother approached us. Loupe said, "Esta bien." "It's all right." Those young men could communicate more with a glance, and a few simple words, than most people could with thousands.

This most important exchange that I would ever have with my friend ended with his painful statement, "I'm sorry, Father, but I've never fallen in love with *your* country." That's one lost love that cost us all.

On October 12, 1999, there was a pink phone note taped to my door. "Loupe called from Mexico. He will be ordained to the deaconate on November 21. He wants you to be there. This is your invitation."

I have no answers to the problems of illegal immigration. My gut feeling is that these people do more good for us than harm. I wish there were some way to protect our own unskilled workers from unfair competition. I also wish there were some way to protect illegal immigrants from working for slave wages and under inhuman conditions. I wish that families did not have to live in constant fear of deportation, or of being divided by an imaginary line in the sand. I wish that honesty could be introduced into the discussion concerning immigration. We need more entry-level workers. There seems to be an unlimited supply of them, south of our border. I wish so many painful things would go away, but until all that happens, our Church has to remain what it has always been, *Catholic.*

When it becomes difficult reconciling the civil law with that divine mandate, may I be radical enough to suggest that our citizenship in the *Kingdom* comes first. Every baptized member of our family is an equal member of our Church. It is not generosity on our part to recognize this. Full participation in the Church is the right of every baptized Catholic. New Catholic parishioners who join well-established parishes are not just tolerated, or condescendingly invited to take part in *our* parish. We can not demand that they be Catholic, in the same way we are. They may not support bingo or fund raisers or use Sunday envelopes. They may not even, immediately, learn our language. Our own ancestors often took more than three generations to become English-speaking. Newcomers deserve the same latitude. Color, language, or legal status can not change the everlasting truths of our faith. There is one Lord, one Faith, and one Baptism. There is one people, who make up the Body of Christ. No manmade law can be allowed to divide that Body. Saying that is easy. Living that means paying a price. Being a real Christian always does.

Post Script: The Ordination

The oath to live a celibate life is a private act of faith in God. It is so personal that it is seldom seen. In the eighteen years that I have been a priest I have only witnessed one other celibacy oath. That was Loupe's brother. Once again, I was invited to watch as my dear friend made his promise to God. After Loupe had sworn that he believed all that the Church teaches he offered himself in sacrifice to God. When he and the young men about to be ordained with him finished reading the words that would change the way they lived for the rest of their lives there was a profound moment of silence. Then the Bishop called my name.

I was completely caught off guard. Bishop Carlos gave me the incredible privilege of signing in witness to the oaths.

The next morning the cathedral was full to capacity hours before the ordinations. The main aisle was jammed with people, as were the side aisles. Worshipers were clustered around the doorways. Even the area in front of the sanctuary was full. Small children used up the remaining space by sitting on the steps in front of the altar. The choir and the concelebrating priests made use of every inch of space behind the altar.

The people knew all of the songs by heart. No one fumbled for books. No one simply mouthed the singing. This was a moment of unrestrained joy for the entire diocese, a good part of which had assembled before us.

The bishop's hands were laid on Loupe's head. He arose a new man. Those chosen to vest the newly ordained deacons approached their parents to receive the dalmatics and stoles. Loupe's brother, Padre Ascension, firmly took my hand. He spoke very little English. However, he managed to say, "We will do this together". I had the honor of placing the stole on my friend. His priest brother vested him in the dalmatic. Of all the undeserved honors I have ever received, this was the most deeply rewarding.

Padre Loupe will become a priest in April of 2000. May God make me more worthy to share our sacrament.

BONE 5

Blessings

Bless Me Father

Sometimes I catch myself doing things simply because I have always seen them done. I do not know why I do such things. They just feel right. Nevertheless, since it is the mission of every believer to make his faith known to the non-believer, it is important to know the meaning behind ritual actions.

When I was a child, I served mass. So many of the questions asked today were not even thought of back then. Priests were men. That was not challenged. Servers were boys. Sisters never seemed to age. Life may not have been better, but it definitely was simpler.

After every mass, I went to the priest and asked for his blessing. I usually got a wave of the hand and a few mumbled words. More often than not, the priest didn't even look in my direction as he pronounced the blessing. I do not know why I remember these moments with such fond satisfaction.

After I was ordained, I continued the custom that I had known as a child of blessing the altar servers. This surprised the boys at my parish. The other priests at my parish had given up this practice. I did not know that I was unique in blessing the boys who served mass. In fact, I knew little of what my brother priests were doing when they celebrated early morning mass. I did what I had always known as a child, assuming that it was still a widespread custom.

I was a little surprised, when a few years later, some of those boys who had since become young men told me that the blessings

I had given them after morning mass were among their fondest memories of growing up. They also told me that when I was transferred to another parish, the priest who followed me refused to give them a blessing unless they could tell him what it meant. They could no more verbalize the implied significance of this simple liturgical ritual, than they could explain the meaning of transubstantiation, predestination, or election. It just felt right, and they missed it.

They made it important for me to be able to explain why priests bless anyone or anything. The roots are found in Scripture and the human heart.

In the sixth chapter of Numbers, Jewish priests were given two hereditary privileges. They were to offer the sacrifices to God, and bless the people with His name. A great deal has been made of the sacrificial offerings of priests. However, the blessings of priests have gained less press.

The heart of Jewish worship has always been the *barakah*. The word is loosely translated, *blessing*. Nineteen Blessings form the core of Jewish synagogue worship. God is blessed, thanked, for His gifts to humanity. At the end of the synagogue liturgy, only a priest is allowed to offer the blessing, recorded in Numbers. He does so, because it is his hereditary right. The priest need display no particular personal piety. It is enough that he is a priest who has reached adulthood. Many pious Jews believe that when he blesses those already joined to God's chosen people with the Name revealed to Moses on Sinai, the light from the Burning Bush, the Shekinah, passes though the openings of his fingers, and is imposed upon the people. The people bow their heads to receive this Divine Presence. To look at the Shekinah would invite the contagion of holiness. To see the glory of God could be fatal. The Jewish Scriptures contain several stories of individuals who saw or touched things they should not have seen or touched. They died.

Belief in God's Presence during the Aaronic Blessing caused the Jewish people to cast down their eyes. Christians who bow their heads are connected, often unknowingly, to their elder Jewish brothers and sisters by this little cultic act of faith in the Presence of the Holy. This ancient gesture of humility springs from the Jewish roots of Christian worship.

Whether in synagogue or church, when God is blessed by a person who speaks with a special cultic authority, the thing or person for whom God is being thanked is recognized as a unique, holy gift from God. That recognition not only identifies, but it also establishes holiness. "Blessed be God for giving you to me to be my friend!" means that you have been sent from God to sanctify my life. The divine gift you are is a blessing from God for me. "Thank God for you!" recognizes who God is as the source and author of all that is good in you, and recognizes who you are as a holy gift from the hand of a gracious God. That very recognition confers what it identifies.

If blessings are nothing more than words, accompanied by hand gestures or splashing water, they lose their significance and their purpose. Anyone can say the words of a blessing, and in a sense every person who thanks God for some gift, human or divine, does invoke a real blessing, with real value. Nevertheless, when the priest speaks on behalf of the entire Church, the living Body of Christ, a kind of consecration takes place that changes the object of the blessing. An individual blesses in his name. An ordained priest blesses in the Name of Almighty God, on behalf of the entire people of God. Once something has been formally blessed, it receives a permanent holiness. For that reason, more in the past than at present, articles that had been blessed by a priest were not sold. When they were no longer usable, they were reverently destroyed or buried. I'm not going to go on some kind of crusade to return to *the good old days,* but a clearer recognition that blessed items deserve greater respect seems more in keeping with the idea the Church is trying to convey.

The significance of a priestly blessing is made clearer through an understanding of the evolution of *barakah,* into the Greek word *eucharistia.* Every time that the Hebrew word, barakah, appears in the Jewish Scriptures, it is translated as eucharistia in Greek. The blessing of God, the expression of gratitude to God in Hebrew, for one of His gifts, becomes the name of the ultimate thanksgiving of the Christian Church, *Eucharist.*

The One God of the Jews is thanked by Christian worshipers, who go to the Father, through the Son, in the Spirit. When the Father is thanked for sending the Son, the action of the Spirit makes the Son present on the altar. The bread and wine offered to the Father as the body and blood of His Son are returned to the people, so that they can enter into communion with the Father. The people then receive the living body, blood, soul, and divinity of the One through whom the Father has been thanked, or in Jewish terms, blessed.

Therefore, it is not entirely incorrect for people to speak of the bread and wine as being *blest* at mass, as long as *blest* is meant in a more profound sense than a simple blessing. The Eucharist is the ultimate Christian Blessing. All other priestly blessings flow from it. To be sure, when a parent blesses a child before bedtime, or a family prays a blessing over a holiday meal, something profoundly holy takes place. But it is the blessing of the priest that is most closely linked to the Blessing that makes Jesus present in a sacramental way. That Blessing is part of the original experience of Jesus. Its roots are sunk into Mount Sinai. It is part of the gift and dignity of priesthood.

Its true meaning can not be expressed in a false democratization. "May God bless us" does not express the gift that is bestowed, or more properly identified, by the priest on behalf of the entire Church.

Therefore, my young friends, you have been the cause of a great part of my joy, and my hope for the future. You bent the direction of my service to God, when it was new and more pliable. You were, and still are, a gift from God, and a special blessing for me. I recognize the holiness that dwells within you, and bless you, Kerry, Mike, Ron, Kyle, Daniel, Chris, Tim, Eddie, Leroy, and Paul, in the name of the Father, and of the Son, and of the Holy Spirit. Amen.

BONE 6

Prayers for the Living and the Dead

The Onion

Once upon a time there was a peasant woman and a very wicked woman she was. And she died and did not leave a single good deed behind. The devils caught her and plunged her into the lake of fire. So her guardian angel stood and wondered what good deed of hers he could remember to tell to God. "She once pulled up an onion in her garden," said he, "and gave it to a beggar woman." And God answered: "You take that onion then, hold it out to her in the lake, and let her take hold and be pulled out. And if you can pull her out of the Lake, let her come to Paradise, but if the onion breaks the woman must stay where she is." The angel ran to the woman and held out the onion to her. "Come," he said, "catch hold and I'll pull you out." And he began cautiously pulling her out. He had just pulled her right out, when the other sinners in the lake, seeing how she was being drawn out, began catching hold of her so as to be pulled out with her. But she was a very wicked woman and she began kicking them. "I'm to be pulled out, not you. It's my onion, not yours." As soon as she said that, the onion broke. And the woman fell into the

> **lake and she is burning there to this day. So the angel
> wept and went away.**
>
> —*Fyodor Dostoyevsky*

Of all the forms of human compassion, giving another person the knowledge that he or she is needed, that his life counts for something, is the most liberating. Individual importance is more than the cornerstone of western political theory. It is at the heart of the message of Jesus Christ. Every individual human person counts. In fact, every individual person is sacred. That makes every choice and activity of a human being valuable. It also means that human acts have a moral dimension: they can be right or wrong.

For Christians, one of the most important things one person can do for another is to pray for him. This does not release a Christian from caring about the physical needs of suffering people. In fact, the contrary is true. Because an individual is worthy of prayer, his life and person become so sacred that Jesus gives us the corollary that we can not love God without loving the people He has given to us for that purpose.

People need our prayers. Conversely, we need theirs. To give a gift we are not willing to receive or claim not to need is to impoverish other people. Christians do not have the luxury of being so selfish as to not need anyone else. Uniquely, Catholic and Orthodox Christians recognize the borders of Church to include every individual living on earth as well as those who have gone before us in death.

The best catechism in the Church is the calendar. Everything the Church teaches is celebrated during the Church year. To live one cycle of the Church year is to enter into the whole mystery of living in Christ. Living the Church year directs every member of the Church to conform his living to what he believes. One of the dogmas of faith, the Communion of Saints, is celebrated at two moments during the Church year—All Saint's Day and All Soul's Day.

All Saint's Day proclaims our reliance on the prayers of those who have gone before us. They have left this earth but still love us and pray to God for us. We assume that they have reached a union with God and are, therefore, able to minister to us through prayer. That is certainly the case for great Christian heroes, Mary the Mother of our Lord and Savior, and the other saints recognized by the Church. However, it also includes those believers who are with God, but who may not be officially recognized as having lived heroic lives while on earth. We count on their love for support in the trials of daily living.

In turn, we pray for those who have died who may still need our help. The minute we admit that the dead can benefit from the prayers and actions of the living and that the living can benefit from the prayers of those who are dead, we proclaim an ecclesiology that pushes the boundaries of the Church into heaven, and a place short of heaven, where people still need help.

Christianity was shattered over this ecclesiology. Martin Luther observed the avaricious exaggerations of this teaching of Church. He correctly observed that no one else could choose for an individual the salvation that Christ alone has earned for him. Death ends the time to choose. He believed that at the moment of death the individual was either saved or lost. There was nothing more that those on earth could do for them. The conflict that followed his theory set into motion the forces that would destroy the unity of European Christianity. Most Catholic theologians see little positive good in picking the scabs off of such old and painful wounds. Nevertheless, praying for the dead and receiving help from those who have died are still part of the Catholic faith.

Early in my priesthood a terrified woman appeared on the front steps of the priest's house. She was wide-eyed. She had a death grip on a five-dollar bill clutched in her right hand.

"Are you a priest?" she asked.

I thought that my black clothes and Roman collar made that clear, but I didn't want to be impolite so I verified the obvious.

"Then here," she said, shoving the five at me.

A little confused by her directness, I invited an explanation, "Why don't you come in and tell me what this is for."

The lady then explained that she was not Catholic. Her neighbors had a daughter who had just been diagnosed with leukemia. The child's family had asked all of the friends of the family to pray to St. Jude, the patron of hopeless causes, for their little girl. That placed this woman and her family in a difficult position. Her heart was breaking for her friends at this time of anguish. She wanted, no, that would not express it, she needed to give her suffering friends the comfort they requested, but neither this woman nor her family believe in the intercessory prayers of saints.

In a courageous act of incredible compassion the woman sought out a priest to help her through the impasse. She ended up at my door. Perhaps, even more courageously she said, "We don't believe in having saints pray for you. So, here, you do it." She shoved the five at me.

"Let me get this straight, you are offering to pay me for doing something that you think is wrong. Is that it? I'm to be your hired, proxy sinner."

"Well, I guess so," she answered. "We really feel bad about our neighbor's little girl. We want to let them know that we are with them during all this."

"Tell me, don't you believe that the apostles of Jesus are alive and in heaven?" I asked.

"Of course!" she replied.

"And you believe that they are just as alive as you or I?"

"Yes."

"And still, you are willing pay me five dollars to ask someone that you believe is really alive and who sees God every day, face to face, to pray for your neighbor. You will ask me to make that request but you will not ask for it yourself. Now, I'll take your five dollars and give it to someone who needs it. But you can still save yourself some money and just talk directly to St. Jude. Every Christian I know thinks highly of the twelve apostles. St. Jude was a charter member of that club."

"No, we don't do that, here."

I took the money. That woman was a kind and decent neighbor. She wanted to do all she could to bring comfort to her friends without sacrificing her religious identity. I appreciated that. Nevertheless, I felt a little sorry for her.

She needed to help. Catholics believe that that need goes both ways and even stretches beyond the grave. Suffering people are easy to love when we can see them before us. It is not so easy when they are far away and we do not know them or they have left this life.

Human beings instinctively know that love does not die just because the one we love has passed from this life. All of the human rites of mourning and burial give evidence of our continued feelings for the dead. We care for their bodies, erect stone monuments to them, and gather on special days to honor their memories.

Catholic and Orthodox Christians go one step further; we express our love in prayers for the dead. We live our belief that our prayers accomplish something for people who have left this world. The concept is based on the idea that we shall not enter heaven broken and scarred, physically or spiritually.

If we were blind or deaf or paralyzed on earth, we will not be so for all eternity in heaven. We will be perfect. Frankly, I do not know what a perfect *me* will look like. I am fairly sure I'll be younger and thinner. I think that my hair will be darker than it is now.

The perfection I hope for will also include a purgation of the spiritual imperfections that have taken root in my life. Before I am allowed into heaven, something will have to be done to increase the level of my prudence. I also expect that the human appetites that I have sometimes allowed to get out of control to become really balanced for the first time. I will no longer think only of myself or nurse old grudges.

I hope that I shall one day see God, face to face. I shall not leave this life perfect enough to walk into heaven, as is. I'll need some fine-tuning and in a few cases a major over-haul. That process will be a free and unmerited gift from God just as much as salvation. I take comfort in believing that the prayers of my brothers and sisters united to the sacrifice of Christ on the cross will somehow miraculously be part of that loving purgation. I do not fear it. I do not dread it.

When I was seven years old, my first grade teacher, a wonderful young sister, told me that I had reached the age of reason. I could now choose to do something so bad that I could merit hell, where I would burn forever. However, if I was sorry for my sins and I had the chance to confess them before I died, then I would only burn in purgatory for a few thousand years or so. Frankly, I remember thinking that if I was going to do the time, I wanted to enjoy the crime.

Sister should have reminded us that words used to explain spiritual realities were just symbols for things that can only be described in a poetic way. We call heaven and hell places, and they are, but you can not get to either one by spaceship or any other means of physical transportation. They do exist but are outside of this created reality. Purgatory is also a place, but not a place like St. Louis, although they do have some things in common. It might even be better symbolized by words like *process* or *purification*. That certainly is the way the Catechism of the Second Vatican Council speaks about this reality.

Whatever we call it, it makes possible a bond that unites us with those we love who still need us. That bond is a celebration of undying love and compassion. It gives the helpless mourner something of great value that he can still do for a person who shared an important part of his life. The existence of purgatory means that the living are still needed by those who have died. We can still give someone we love something they need. We have a purpose. Even motionless in a hospital bed, if we can manage even a momentary kind thought for a loved one, living or dead, our life has meaning. And if, living in the mystery of God, the people we remember in prayer no longer need our acts of love and spiritual sacrifice, God will direct our best efforts as He sees fit. People who have been perfected may not need our help. In that case we rely on their prayers for us.

Some day I'll reach up for an onion my guardian angel is holding out to me. I know that I shall not be able to claim that I have been as compassionate as I could have been. I hope that my onion will hold. If I have remembered to love my brothers and sisters on earth even in death, I shall not be alone when I reach up. With a little help from my friends, I think that my onion may be strong enough to pull several of us into eternal joy. If that is the case, it will be a matter of a great many people, some living on earth and others living in heaven, most of whom I shall never know in this life, nailing their own sacrifices to the foot of the cross with Jesus for me.

Every human act of kindness offered for the benefit of those who have died accomplishes something. The Church identifies some of these acts and confers upon them a special value. Many more are personal and individual. By performing them we open our own lives to a profound effect of the crucifixion. We either help someone we love or we grow in holiness.

Finally, prayers for one who is eternally lost mean that some of us are capable of loving the unlovable. If those prayers are of no use to the one for whom they are intended, then they come back to those who offered them. They are not wasted. No act of love ever is.

The five-dollar bill given by that loving woman for her friend was the only prayer she could unite to that of St. Jude. God, the Great Comedian, must certainly have laughed that day. I am also absolutely sure that a nice lady planted one more tough onion in her garden.

BONE 7

Church

The Community of Believers
Was of One Heart and One Mind

Kerry and Eileen had dated after high school. I thought that my friend had found his future wife. Kerry was one of my dearest friends. I knew that he admired me and had quietly considered my life for himself. However, early in his life he had discovered that God was probably not calling him to the priesthood. We both knew that and were comfortable with it. He was my friend and I wanted nothing more than for him to find the path God had laid out for him.

It really surprised me to hear that Kerry and Eileen had decided not to see each other. I had always liked Eileen. I was convinced that she would make my friend happy. Nevertheless, the love that brings a husband and wife together is a mystery. Not only do the people have to be right for a marriage to work; the timing has to be right. So they broke up, and I still loved them both.

A few years later Kerry was led back to Eileen. She was naturally a bit gun-shy, but she had never really stopped loving my friend. Kerry was ready for *that* question.

Family was important to him. He mapped out a really romantic plan. He wanted to fly to California with Eileen and ask her to become his wife surrounded by aunts, uncles, and family. He also wanted me along. I believe that his exact words were "If she says, 'no,' I'll need a priest." I knew that *no* would not be part of that conversation.

The trip was tenser than I had expected. Kerry and I knew that the big moment would come when the time was right, but neither of us knew when that would be.

Time was running out. Kerry was doing all the right things. He held her hand and even sang country western love songs to her. That had to be real love. Kerry should not sing.

The day before coming home we all went skiing. The world was beautiful. As we climbed the mountains outside of Sacramento, we looked back to see a forest of redwoods poking through the cloud cover. A distant passenger jet seemed to move through the spotless blue sky just over the forest of treetops. Certainly this would be the day!

Midwesterners should never go skiing. It is such a rare treat that we almost always overdo it. That night every muscle that had any strength left to hurt did so. Kerry and I were beyond pain. Every time we moved we hurt. There was nothing to do but call out for God and just laugh.

Eileen slept in the room next door. It is always difficult being left out of the fun. She heard the laughter through the wall and assumed that we were talking about her! Maybe paranoia is unavoidable when you are the odd-man-out. The next morning Eileen was quiet. Kerry and I instantly knew that we had done something wrong. It probably had something to do with being male. Whatever it was, we were guilty—all men know how to recognize that state of being somehow perpetually at fault. I think that it may have something to do with Adam and Eve.

It took several quiet hours in the car before Eileen finally let us know how deeply offended she was that we were talking and laughing about her the night before. I think that Kerry could not have convinced her otherwise, but Eileen was a strong Catholic and was willing to give me the benefit of the doubt. She graciously accepted my assurance that we had not been talking or laughing about her. It didn't really matter. The mood was broken.

Eventually, Kerry found a more private moment to plead his case. As I had suspected, Eileen said, "Yes." That set the stage for the most intimate experience of Christ's sacramental presence in His people I have ever been privileged to witness.

After two years of marriage they were about to be blessed with a child. I counted the days and hours along with my friends. I was given the greatest of honors. I was the first person called when the child arrived.

I don't remember if I cancelled appointments or just missed them. All I know is that I dropped everything and immediately headed for the hospital.

Kerry had finally gone home for a needed shower. Eileen was in her room with *our* little one. By this time I felt like a real grandfather.

Eileen was holding her first-born son when I entered her room. Kerry came back and entered the room seconds behind me, before I had time to say anything. I kissed his young wife on the cheek and then looked her son in the face. He was beautiful!

In the Bauman family, it has never been the custom to give a child the same name as an adult. Each child is his or her own unique person. However, in this case Kerry and Eileen made an exception. Their son was named Christopher Daniel. The Daniel was for me. Christopher is to still grow up his own man, but we share the same middle name.

Kerry walked over to the edge of the bed. Without words Eileen handed their child to his father. The most beautiful thing I had ever seen was about to take place. It was not the incredible vision of mother and child; it was not even the tender look on the face of a father the first time I saw him hold his child. The thing that still overwhelms me, the high point of my sacramental life was seeing the look on Eileen's face the first time she watched her husband hold their child and love him. There could be no greater look of contentment and affection than the one I saw at that moment.

I do not understand people who define religion without that kind of passion. God is love. Is it so hard to understand that it is reflected, sometimes almost perfectly, in the love we have for each other? This has to be what Jesus meant when He said, "Where two or three are gathered in my name, there I am among them."

Many people have tried to define *Church*. I witnessed it on a woman's face and cradled in a man's arms.

A have another friend who is an ordained minister. He is the pastor of a Pentecostal congregation. His business cards have a slogan on them, "'The Church is Not the Building. The Church is the People." I love my friend but I disagree with him. The Church is not the building, but in saying that "The Church is the People," he is leaving Someone out. The Church is not just the total of its members. It is not a club or fraternity. It is the people of God, but only when God lives in them. Without God, the people are not the Church. They are only a group of people who believe the same things.

The people with God living in them, the Church, can do things that only God can do. It can forgive sins, love the unlovable, and bestow salvation on people with a little water and words of faith. Its members can become part of a Body that includes total strangers. It can change ordinary bread and wine into the living Body, Blood, Soul, and Divinity of Jesus. In short, when people allow themselves to be Church, they can walk on water. Words have to be found to present that sublime mystery to the world.

We live in a reductionist age. Politicians and salesmen try to communicate through sound bites. Even great ideas are reduced to slogans. There is a tendency to strip away all that is superfluous in the hope of discovering the essentials. It should not surprise us that this has also become one of the most popular approaches to religion and the Church.

The paradigm for this ecclesiology is the noble peach. The essence of all that a peach is and can become is found in the seed. To get at it one has to strip away the fuzz, the peel, and even the flesh. The seed contains within it thousands of peaches, forests of trees, and therefore a kind of immortality. Some future human being, living at the end of the fourth millenium may enjoy a peach from a tree that can be traced back to this single seed. All that a peach is and may become is mysteriously contained in that seed. Rip away the non-essentials and discard them if you really want to get at the mystery.

That is precisely how many people search for Jesus and the meaning of His Church. They see the layers of history and tradition as hindrances in the way of knowing the *real* Jesus. The only church of interest to them is the simple church of the apostles. Anything else is a distraction. They seek one *peach* of a church. Unfortunately, they will most probably never find it. They can imagine one that comfortably fits what they hope to find, but the real Church can no more be discovered in this radical reductionist way than a great painting can be discovered by removing all its colors.

The truth is that the search for Jesus has more in common with peeling an onion than in removing the flesh of a peach. Jesus is not found at the center of the onion. He is contained in its layers. He is present in the Wisdom of Sacred Scripture, even the difficult passages that seem to stand in the way of things I may want. This is the closest layer to the center, but it is not the center.

Jesus is found in the liturgies, the practices of the people, the laws, the leadership, and the entire lived experience of what the Church is in human history. Each layer contains something of the mystery. If each of these layers is cut away and discarded, the mystery of Jesus and His Church are thrown away in the process. When all of these layers are gone and the center of the onion is reached, all that is left is a handful of stink that will make you cry.

The mystery of Christ can not be separated from the mystery of the Church. Just as Jesus was both human and divine, the Church is both human and divine. The difference between Jesus and His Church is that He was a man like us in all things, except sin. The Church is human in all things, *including* sin. Jesus never sinned. The Church does.

To expect the Church to be too good is to deny its humanity. That would be a distortion of one of its two natures. Expecting the Church to be more perfect than it can be is one of the oldest and most pernicious of heresies. The Church was not strict enough for the Donatists who refused to forgive some kinds of sins. It was not pure enough for the Catharists who demanded that its *perfect ones* live like angels. It was not scientific enough for the Rationalists or simple enough for the Fundamentalists.

The Church sometimes sins. I'm not speaking about the more notorious things people are always bringing up—the crusades, inquisitions, persecutions, and social injustices. When I say that the Church sins, I mean the daily things that are sometimes done in its name which are directly opposed to the spirit of its Founder.

Frankly, I wish I could open a book and read that just before the fire was lighted to burn St. Joan of Arc, some bishop changed his mind and shouted, "Release her! She is not guilty!" I wish that some priest had refused to condemn Jewish families to murder or deportation from Spain. I wish that someone had defended Galileo's right to think and teach. I wish that some pope had condemned slavery long before the Western Hemisphere was even known to exist, thus removing the cause of our Civil War before it could fester and come to a head. I wish that revolutions and wars of liberation had been made unnecessary centuries ago by a Church that insisted on Christ's peace, love, and justice. I can wish for all of those things. It does no good at all. They did not happen. Perhaps they should have, but the Church left to us by Jesus is human and can sin.

Yet that Church is also divine. It has kept the fire of compassion alive in the longings of its suffering saints. It has surrounded hope with a rationale. It has never completely lost the light of its faith. Sometimes in spite of itself, it has been the only way to soften the brutality of human greed. It may not have condemned slavery early enough, but it did not stop St.Vincent de Paul from selling himself into slavery to buy a brother's freedom. It may not have been able to speak out more forcefully against the holocaust, but it did not stop St. Maximillian Kolbe from offering his life in place of that of a condemned man. It has ordered the burning of books and the suppression of ideas, only to provide a place for them to survive in monastery libraries and great universities.

The Church has sinned. It has also been the healing presence of Compassion. Its children must always find the courage to speak out against injustice, even if the injustice is from time to time found in the Church. However, it must also be remembered that destroying the peace of the Church is itself a form of injustice. Before troubling the waters to demand justice from the Church, every other effort has to be exhausted first. Making a tear in the seamless garment of Christ is not to be lightly considered. Before the demand is made, the proportionality between the good hoped for and the damage that might possibly result has to be weighed and considered. As long as the Church is made up of people who sin, even when they are united by the presence of God, the Church will have two natures, one human and the other divine. It will continue to have the ability to sin until the day of its glorification when human history ends in eternity. I have seen a glimpse of that day on a new mother's face.

BONE 8

Confession

My Peace,
Is my gift to you

When I was a child, my father liked to make his own beer. It wasn't especially good beer, but he really seemed to like making it. I still remember the recipe. Seven gallons of water, a five pound bag of sugar, a can of barley malt, a cake of yeast, and a few cut up potatoes or a bag of rice were mixed together in a stone crock and left in a warm place for a few days. Every few hours dad skimmed the scum off of the top of the fermenting brew. When he could shine his flashlight into the beer and see that the yeast had just about finished working, he bottled it in used bottles. Just before capping the stuff, we put about a teaspoon full of sugar in each bottle. That made the yeast continue to work just enough to build up carbonation in the beer, making it foamy.

Dad's beer making was never very sophisticated; however, there was more of an art to it than one might think. One of his newly bottled batches had appeared to stop working during a short cold spell. The night he bottled that beer, which just happened to be during the Cuban missile crisis, the weather turned warm and every bottle of new beer exploded. The worst part of it was that as each bottle blew up it first whistled like an incoming bomb. That night I was awakened to the sound of exploding beer bombs. Somewhere between deep sleep and being blown wide-awake, I prayed my first perfect act of contrition.

Helping dad with his beer was one of those bonding things between father and son. I always liked doing things with my dad, and I enjoyed seeing the pride on his face when he offered a bottle of his homemade beer to a friend. The recipe and process was so easy that I was sure I could imitate it if I needed to.

In the summer between high school and college, my parents took the first real vacation they had ever had. They drove to Texas to see my uncle. I had a summer job and had to stay behind *house sitting*. Every parent knows the last words I heard my mother say as the family pulled out of the driveway, "We trust you! Be careful! Good-bye! Remember, no parties!"

I immediately got on the phone to plan the first party. I have to say up front that I was not really much of a problem to my parents when I was growing up. I was born in 1947 and grew up in the conformist fifties. I mostly did what I was told and took well to discipline. Drugs and teen pregnancies were not something I had to consider. I tried hard not to break the law. Since underage drinking was against the law, I avoided it.

None of that meant anything when I saw my parents pull out of the driveway and I was on my own for the first time in my life. I went to the basement and got out the beer crock. With the help of my friends from school, I mixed the forbidden brew and the wait was on.

Three days later we bottled our first batch of home brew. It looked like beer, smelled like beer, and foamed like beer.

The following Saturday every kid I knew came to my house for the official tasting. I had the honor of going first. I took a big lusty pull off the first foaming bottle of cold home brew. It was totally and absolutely the worst thing I had ever put into my mouth! Something had gone very wrong.

It didn't take long for most of my friends to find a polite excuse to leave my non-party. Only my partners in crime remained to pour out the offending swill. The party had really not taken place, and the evidence had been destroyed. My guardian angel, or maybe it had been a direct intervention of God, had kept me from successfully completing my first act of adolescent rebellion. Except for my new unpopularity no real harm had been done, and my folks *would never find out*.

As with all great plans, this one had one fatal flaw. Toward the end of the bottling process we had run out of bottles. Instead of pouring out the little beer that remained, I had decided to pour it into three fruit jars and store it in the bottom of my closet for later use. We destroyed all the evidence of our unlawful project except those three jars of rot gut beer. They lay, forgotten, under some dirty clothes in the bottom of my closet. I left for college that fall. I was the first person in my family to attend high school, the first to graduate, and the first to go to college. My parents were so proud!

When I left, my brother Steve began to cry. Then the thought that he would get my room somehow seemed to compensate for my leaving. The family was still intact but divided. That's life!

My mother, perhaps feeling the loss of my presence in the house, did something she hadn't done in years. She cleaned my room. Yes, she also cleaned the closet, and, yes, she found my stash.

I'll never forget the letter she sent to me, her eldest and dearest son. The words of her terse note seemed to burn off the page. She used words uncharacteristic for her, words like *filthy,* and *disgusting*, and *pig!* Overall I thought her reaction was somewhat excessive. Then I finished the short letter.

Mom had not found my beer. She found what she thought was the disgusting result of my laziness in using fruit jars for thunder mugs! She thought my beer was human waste and I was filthy enough to store it in the bottom of my closet. No wonder she was so steamed!

Now I was faced with a real dilemma. She already thought her oldest son was a disgusting slob. Should I tell her that my hygiene was not really that bad and admit that I was a disobedient, untrustworthy, teenage brewmeister? Slob or drunk, which did I want my mother to think of me.

When I made it home for Thanksgiving, my dad was waiting for me on the front porch. "Nice batch you made," were the first words out of his mouth.

"What?" said I, affecting total innocence.

"Your beer," said dad, "it tasted pretty good."

"But dad, how did you know that it was beer?"

"Well, son, when your mother made me carry it to the back of the yard and pour it out next to the fence, I tasted it and it wasn't bad."

"You tasted it? Didn't you think that it was what mom thought it was?"

"Well, yes, at first, but when I began to pour it out, I smelled it and decided to give it a try. It was beer, all right, and a pretty good batch."

"Does mom know?"

"Are you out of your mind! She'd just blame me for teaching you how to make the stuff. We'd better leave this alone."

"You know, dad, I never did get to drink any of that beer. When I tried it, it tasted horrible. I had to pour most of it out."

"Your real mistake was trying to drink it before it had time to settle. Green beer is always bitter. After a few weeks it's fine."

"Am I in trouble?"

"Not with me, but there's going to be hell to pay with your mother. I figure that will be punishment enough."

My mother went to her grave believing that her son was a dirty, filthy pig, capable of urinating in fruit jars and storing them in his closet. I never got around to explaining the truth to her, even after I had rehabilitated my reputation by becoming a priest. In the end that was my punishment.

In my house forgiveness was a way of life. Every child should have parents who are always there, who sometimes show anger, but who never turn their backs on the people they love the most. When the nuns began to teach me about God as my Father, I knew exactly about whom they were talking. My father loved me, even when I had done wrong. My mother loved me too, but she did have a little shorter fuse.

Growing up, I never felt abandoned. I knew that things were expected of me, and I sometimes disappointed my folks. Yet, I can't think of a single time when I doubted, even for a moment, that they would forgive me and continue loving me, no matter what I did. It was easy for me to know who God was. I had seen such a wonderful reflection of His presence in the parents He gave me.

I still like parties—nowadays I don't have to make the liquid refreshment! I enjoy being with friends and relaxing over a cold beer and getting into discussions about things that really matter. Unfortunately every party has a quota of one obnoxious person with bad breath. He is the guy who loves to back the priest into a corner and begin telling him what is wrong with the Church. This guy may not really be a jerk but a little beer seems to bring out the worst in him. He usually likes poking the priest in the chest with his finger as he recounts the usual list of things that we can all do without.

Somewhere in the top five things wrong with the Catholic Church will be confessing sins to a priest. Usually more eloquent after at least three beers, the drooling prophet will explain to me that he does not need to tell his sins to a priest. He can tell them directly to God. Not only that! He can also find God in the mountains or out in the forest and he, therefore, does not need to go to Church.

What a revelation! You mean that it is actually possible for an individual to *talk* directly to God! What sublime insight! What a monumental breakthrough! Imagine that, an ordinary person can actually speak directly to God! I wonder what the world will call this when news of it gets out. Do you think that it might be called prayer?

Back in the fourth century Origen preached a homily based on Leviticus. In it he identified eight different ways of having one's sins forgiven: baptism, martyrdom, almsgiving, forgiving one who has sinned against you, converting a sinner, acts of charity, confession to a priest, and the anointing of the sick. All of this has been spelled out since the fourth century. Still, people keep reinventing the wheel and discovering that there are, indeed, ways of being forgiven by God other than by going to confession. The Church has always known that and never suggested that sacramental confession was the one and only way to receive God's forgiveness.

I hope that every member of our Church knows how to make an act of contrition and uses it often. I also hope that individuals do find God in the forest, in the mountains, on the oceans, and anywhere else that the glory and beauty of God are reflected in nature. I certainly find Him there.

Our Church draws a distinction between Revelation and inspiration. Revelation is the Word of the Father. It is essentially Jesus. Jesus is all that the Father has ever wanted to say to the world. In that Word lies all the compassion and hope God can give us. We can have that Word. We can really accept Him into our lives. We call the unique and real presences of Jesus *sacraments.* There are seven of them.

We come to the Church to find Jesus and then to receive Him. He can be there in the mystery of God's forgiveness. We can have forgiveness in a number of ways including going to our room, closing the door, and asking for God's forgiveness. That forgiveness is real. However, we can have something more. We can have Jesus in sacrament.

Every sacrament is an encounter with Jesus. He has willed to be with us, until the end of time. Seeking only God's forgiveness, without receiving the sacramental presence of His Son, denies ourselves a great source of strength and peace.

Mere forgiveness, alone, is so small compared to the presence of Jesus. Those who approach the sacrament of reconciliation present themselves for special communion with God. Where God dwells, sin can not exist, but that is not all that God's presence means. There is not a single longing of the human heart that is not filled to capacity and beyond by the presence of God.

I pity those who seek only forgiveness, when they can have so much more. They can be filled with the source of every hope, belief, and love. They can have Jesus. All they have to do is come to Him and empty themselves, so that He has room to work.

The sacrament of reconciliation is not an exercise in humiliation. It is a way of accepting the peace and strength that God desires to give us. It is not a denial of the evil we have done. It is the opposite of denial. It is honest, radical acceptance of the responsibility for the choices made in life. It is also the recognition that some of those choices have been the wrong ones. It is the means of laying down debilitating guilt for what has been done. It is a way out of the pit. It is freedom from the burden—a way to keep living, and to recapture the joy of being alive.

I suspect that any human being who has ever needed to hear the words *you are forgiven* understands why sins have to be said out loud. Likewise, anyone who has never needed to hear those words will never understand anything about the confession of sins.

I love to read and study, but everything I know about laying down life's burdens, and the joy of living, I learned from my family. They taught by forgiving. I learned by being forgiven.

BONE 9

Celibacy

For the Sake of the Kingdom

On a number of occasions I have been confronted by people who express the opinion that the Church ought to allow me to get married. My response to such people has always been "What have I ever done to you?"

Marriage is a beautiful gift from God. There is nothing else that provides two people with the support and grace that the sacrament of marriage offers. However, marriage is not a gift I have been given. I am quite content with the one I have accepted in its place. I am a celibate priest.

I am not, as I have heard said, an unmarried male. I am a celibate man. I do not believe that I can remain celibate if I have a sexual relationship outside of marriage. I can not be a celibate and at the same time be a bachelor on the prowl, cruising single's bars. My celibacy can not be reduced to merely refraining from marriage. I am determined to live my life in absolute and perpetual continence. That means no sex with anyone, ever.

I want everyone to understand that this is the life I have freely chosen. I did not have to take a promise of celibacy. I did not have to be ordained a priest. I chose both of these gifts because, for me, either one would have been meaningless without the other.

Everything in this culture is worth what someone is willing to pay for it. Because I consider priesthood such an incredible treasure, I am willing to pay my sex life for it. In fact, even that statement fails to capture the value of what I am willing to pay for priesthood. Celibacy means a great deal more than no sex. It also means growing old without the comfort of a life-long partner and without children or grandchildren. It may even mean accepting an element of loneliness. However, in truth, I have not experienced a great deal of that.

I live in a country in which eighteen-year-old boys are asked to put their lives on the line for their country. They are asked to risk a lot more than their potential family lives, and for something worth a great deal less than their faith in God. Millions of young people have responded to that request. Why, then, is it considered inhuman to ask the same young men to accept celibacy as a response to priesthood?

Frankly, I am not gratified when someone degrades the life I have chosen. I honor marriage and respect those who have committed themselves to it. I expect the same respect for my own way of life, especially from Catholics. I consider it rude of people to assume that I hate my life and am chomping at the bit to be free of it.

My celibacy is a small gift that I have given to my God. It is only a human gift and it is insignificant compared to that of Jesus on the cross. Nevertheless, it is the gift I have to offer. It is valuable to me. It is important to me. It is my gift to withhold, and mine to give. It is the most intense *I love you* that I can personally offer to the God who taught me to love by emptying Himself for me. I resent having it attacked. I respect honest disagreement concerning the wisdom of making celibacy mandatory for priests. However, I do not enjoy having my gift to God held in contempt.

Sometimes I think that I am addicted to radical honesty. That's probably not a virtue, and I certainly often lack prudence in exercising it. Nevertheless, the whole discussion concerning mandatory clerical celibacy is characterized by some of the most dishonest exchanges I have ever heard.

Many things are approached in a dishonest way at the end of the second millenium. The same Church that requires clerical celibacy is often blamed for world over-population. I would find that laughable, if it were not believed by so many otherwise seemingly intelligent people.

The world reached six billion people in the middle of October, 1999. A child in Catholic Croatia was identified, only God and the United Nations knows how, as the official record breaker. In the minds of many people, that is personally the fault of Pope John Paul II. Never mind the fact that one billion of those people live in Hindu India and don't care what the pope believes about anything. Another two billion live in China, where union with the Church of Rome is illegal. Not many of them consider the words of Pope John Paul when planning their families. Most people in Japan, Singapore, Indonesia, Egypt and, in fact, the entire Islamic world, live their lives without the slightest concern for what the pope thinks about the choices they make in their private lives. Yet, the pope, who promotes sexual abstinence for the unmarried and vowed celibacy for priests and religious, gets the blame for overpopulation, pollution, and poverty.

The truth is that most of the Christian parts of the world are not growing as fast as the non-Christian parts of the world. It is a mystery to me why the Catholic Church is the villain in all of this.

Similarly, many dishonest arguments are employed in attacking the value of clerical celibacy. It astonishes me that many of the same people who blame the pope for overpopulation want priests to have the opportunity to add to that population.

The declining number of priests in Western Europe and the United States is blamed on celibacy. Those who leave the active ministry often make that claim. However, celibacy is only one of the ascetical practices presently under attack. Fasting and abstinence from meat are no more popular than celibacy. They are just more temporary. Any day now, I expect tooth decay to also be blamed on celibacy. None of this makes any sense.

Once again, the truth is that proportionally more priests are loyal to their commitment than married people are to theirs. Nearly half of all Catholic marriages in America end in divorce. I think that eclipses the percentage of priests who walk away from the vocation they have vowed to live. Yet, I hear very few people suggesting that the Church should make fidelity in marriage optional.

The end of clerical celibacy is proposed as the answer to all of the problems faced by the contemporary Church. However, many other traditional Christian denominations have a married clergy, and many of them are not thriving. The marriage of their clergy has not made their future any more sound.

Our Orthodox brothers and sisters ordain married men to the priesthood, as do many of the Eastern Rites of our Catholic Church. However, they do not allow those already ordained to marry, and they do not allow the remarriage of widowed priests or priests who divorce their wives. Since the Orthodox Church ordains men as young as twenty-one, many of their priests marry in their late teens. The teen marriages of future priests end up with many of the same pressures as any other teen marriages. Often when an Orthodox priest's marriage ends in divorce, the priest also loses his ministry through remarriage.

There are good reasons to consider allowing Catholic priests to marry. There are also good reasons for retaining the traditional practice of requiring clerical celibacy. I have no desire to inflict any kind of guilt on a priest who has left the priesthood because he has fallen in love with a woman. I do not think that I am any less sympathetic to them than I am to married men who have fallen in love with women other than their wives. The pain of desiring, perhaps even needing, an illicit love can be very real. Living a vow that no longer gives comfort can make a man bitter. I do not enjoy seeing any human being suffer, but people of integrity are expected to be honorable, even when that is painful; even when it requires great heroism.

Before 313 the Church was not able to legislate much. During the dark period of persecution, it was far too concerned with survival to fine-tune its dogma or its discipline. However, there are some indications that celibacy was already a highly valued practice before the end of the second century.

De Singularitate Clericorum was written sometime early in the third century. It has long been attributed to St. Cyril of Alexandria. That is significant for two reasons. First, in Egypt celibacy was valued. However, Egypt was part of the Greek-speaking world. In the Greek Christian world, celibacy has historically been located in the episcopacy and in monastic communities. This letter recommends celibacy for all of the Egyptian clergy. The second reason that the Egyptian connection is important is precisely because it is distinctly non-Latin. In fact, celibacy has been considered a valuable response to belief in the crucified Christ in every branch of early Christianity: Latin, Greek, and Syriac. In his letter, Cyril did not demand celibacy, but he did strongly recommend it, and seemed scandalized that some clerics were not practicing it.

As the Church began to emerge from persecution, it began to codify many of its long-held practices. In 306 the Synod of Elvira forbade deacons, priests, and bishops from exercising their sexual rights as married men. While this was the first legislative sex-discipline for clerics, it was hardly an innovation. The Synod of Elvira was conservative in every way. It looked to the past for codification and avoided any innovations. It is most probable that it merely legalized long established practice, fine tuning clerical life around the fringes.

In 314 the Synod of Ancyra prohibited deacons who had not formerly declared their intention to marry at the time of their ordinations from doing so. Inasmuch as the Church has always considered such issues as celibacy within the context of hierarchy, it is likely that priests and bishops were expected not even to consider the option offered to those deacons who retained the privilege to marry.

In 390 the second Synod of Carthage added greater weight to the Latin insistence upon clerical celibacy. It was simply assumed for bishops, priests, and deacons and recognized in canon 2 of that Synod. The Synods of Turin, Toledo, Orange, Rome, Tours, Agde, Arles and Carthage are a few of the synods that issued local legislation regarding clerical celibacy, recognizing what had already become venerable custom. Nevertheless, the very necessity of frequent legislation indicated how difficult celibacy was to enforce.

Pope Gregory I wrote extensively concerning the Roman legislation mandating celibacy for his metropolitan area. His insistence upon clerical continence was, perhaps, linked to his monastic approach to the Church. Nevertheless, his discipline formed the background for Western legal codification of clerical celibacy.

The Lateran Synod of 769 recognized the development of an Oriental tradition of married priests, which differed from that which had become normative in the Latin West. That difference has remained in place to this day for priests. Bishops are required to be celibate in both traditions.

Numerous Ecumenical Councils of the Church and many more papal pronouncements defended the Latin practice of mandatory celibacy for priests. To claim that Western clerical celibacy is a late invention is preposterous. It is true that it had to be legislated in many areas over a long period of time. That indicates the difficulty of observing it. It does not lessen its value. However, law does not present a complete picture of the value of anything.

What is the value of celibacy at the beginning of the third millenium? Nothing could be more counter-cultural in the industrial West than celibacy. It goes against the basic assumption underlying the profit incentive of capitalism that a person should be able to have anything he can afford.

The value of celibacy can not be seen, weighed, or sold. It is entirely spiritual. It does not appear pragmatic in any way. It seems to do no practical good for those who practice it or for those who are served by celibates. American Catholics live in a Protestant country, surrounded by denominations with married clergy who function quite effectively.

Celibacy seems valueless to people who believe that a handful of money should be able to solve any problem. If a disease can not be totally eradicated, it is the government's fault for not spending enough money to do the job. If someone ends up pregnant, it is a right to make it all go away for a price. Everything in our culture seems to be about money. Cynical people even believe that clerical celibacy is about cheap labor for the Church, and a guarantee that Church property will not end up willed to family members.

Everyone in America is bombarded with sound bites that proclaim that they should deny themselves nothing. In fact, spending for wanted luxury items *sets you free, makes life worth living,* and *saves.* For Christians, Jesus used to do those things. Now, the things a person can buy are sometimes said to do those things.

In such a world, a lived homily proclaiming that human dignity does not depend on the things one can appropriate to himself—even good things, even things he has every right to have—is a powerful witness.

This life is not all there is to being human. There is a life to come. Therefore, a person can deny himself some of the good things this world has to offer, with the firm conviction that self-denial will mean something in eternity.

Celibacy is one of those publicly lived homilies. The Church does not expect or even want every one to be celibate. However, a few of its most public members are required to be celibate to witness to the reality of spiritual things. Celibates are sometimes lonely. They are often frustrated. They sometimes even fail. Celibacy is not romantic, and certainly not fun. It will not keep a person warm at night. The shortage of men who are willing to accept it testifies to its relative difficulty. It is more difficult to live than married life, at least for most people.

Not everything has to be pragmatic. Not everything of value costs money or can be sold. Not every desire has to be indulged. It is possible for some people to live in a way that proclaims that this life is not an end in itself. I know that and live that because I deny myself something that is good. In fact, marriage is a human right that no one has a right to take away from me. I freely offer my human right to marry to my God. I do this united with brothers. This is our bond and our combined witness. I readily forgive any brother who cannot accomplish what he has publicly promised to do. I pray for every struggling priest. I thank God for each of my brother priests, who make me proud to identify myself as one of their number.

Perhaps, one day, celibacy will no longer be counter-cultural. Perhaps, most people will want the freedom that attends a solitary life. Perhaps, on that day, celibacy will no longer proclaim anything to the world. Then, and only then, it may make sense to abandon its practice. Until that day comes, it remains a testament to the faith of the Church that there is a resurrection of the dead and a life after this one.

BONE 10

The All-Male Priesthood

Gnosticism

The Church had competition during its formative period. Gnosticism was a rival religion, as diverse in character as the new Christian faith. One of its primary tenets was that the created world was evil. Only spiritual realities had any value.

This worldview proposed two gods, one good and the other evil. The appeal of such a system was that it appeared to work. Jews and Christians had as much difficulty in the first century as they do today in explaining how an all-powerful God could allow so many bad things to happen to good people.

Gnosticism had no difficulty on this point. There was a good god and a bad one. The good god gets credit for all that is noble, decent, and good. The evil god gets all the blame for whatever goes wrong. That's about as simple as a system can be.

There were a number of forms of Gnosticism. Some of them were very simple, bordering on popular superstition. Other forms were quite philosophical and complex. Nevertheless, they all rested upon the premise that there were two gods.

Most Gnostics were syncretistic. They freely borrowed any myths or local expressions of religion and baptized them into their own worldview. Judaism and Christianity were challenged in this way. Gnostics identified the God of the Hebrew Scriptures, the Father, as the vengeful god of created matter. This handy explanation rationalized away any violence or capriciousness that seemed to spring from the god who had created the world in six days. Of course, this god commanded Moses to murder helpless women and children captured in battle. He was the evil god, and his book, the Old Testament, was just as evil as he was. Of course, Job was the victim of an elaborate chess game between Lucifer and the god of creation. The Gnostic god of the Hebrew Scriptures enjoyed inflicting that kind of pain for amusement. The world was a giant ant farm and god really enjoyed seeing the ants squirm.

There was a way out of all this misery. The god of the Christian Scriptures was the god of the spirit. He was given the name Jesus. His book was good, but only the elite few knew the secret of what it meant. They alone possessed the wisdom, the gnosis, to know the mind of the good god. The good god of the Gnostics had little in common with the Divine Person of the same name worshiped by Christians. The Gnostic Jesus was at war with the evil god of creation. To ally oneself with this god of the spiritual plane, one had to deny the created impulse whenever possible. Food, drink, even water for bathing was part of the created world of the evil god. It was to be avoided whenever possible. In this elaborate system suicide was highly reverenced. It was the ultimate alliance with the enemy of created matter. Contacting pneumonia by taking a hot bath and standing naked in the cold was a favorite vehicle for Gnostic suicide in parts of Europe with a nasty winter climate. Jumping into large fires was more dramatic and more common in warmer places.

Sex held a special place of contempt for Gnostics. It was seen as a way of adding to the created world. It enlarged the kingdom of creation, of evil. Bringing more created matter into existence was the easiest way of joining the forces of darkness. Of course, in more philosophical Gnostic circles, since created matter was held in such general contempt, it really did not matter at all. Therefore, in some places sex was held in such low esteem that it was given free license. Some of these folks could have it both ways. Sex was an evil vehicle of creation and at the same time lacking any significance because it belonged to the base animal nature and could therefore take place without the slightest dignity or respect. As long as it was held in contempt, those on the way to perfection could have all the sex they wanted. It just didn't matter.

The body was treated with as much disdain as possible. It was beaten, starved, and left unwashed or washed in urine. A gathering of these folks had to have a certain distinct *air* about them.

The Gnostic ideal was to eventually reach a point at which all created matter was completely rejected. There were individuals who seemed to reach that point. They seemed to live without any of the things that made life possible. They wandered in rags and seemed to eat or drink nothing. As perfect ones they avoided the differences between men and women with condescension. Their life was not an easy one. It was so difficult that a Gnostic who happened to come near to death might be joined to their number while very sick and even unconscious. In the event of his recovery the reluctant *perfecti* was recognized as too weak to live his new spiritual state and helped to unwillingly commit *suicide* by loving friends.

This system appears so incredible on the surface that one wonders why it had such a wide appeal. Part of the answer for that can be found in the general religious vacuum of the Roman Empire during the apostolic period. The old answers simply no longer worked. No matter how much incense was burned or no matter how many sacrifices were made to gods, the outcome of life's constant dramas never seemed to be altered. At least Gnosticism had answers. Two gods at war made sense. All that a human being had to do was decide which side he was on and allow all future consequences to flow from that decision.

Some elements of Gnosticism seeped into localized expressions of Christianity. At times it is difficult to know for sure whether a particular document is an ancient Christian document tinged with Gnosticism or a Gnostic document tinged with Christianity. Persecution does those kinds of things. It drives schools of thought underground where they can not easily be identified with absolute precision.

Some of the anti-body and anti-sex Gnostic worldview did have an effect on early Christian communities, especially in the East. For a time, the Syriac Church required absolute celibacy as a requirement for anyone seeking baptism. This is reflected in the Gospel and Acts of Thomas. Sex was called the *garment of shame* and was to be *trampled under foot.* This discipline was condemned at the Council of Nicaea, thus making it possible for the Syriac Church to survive.

However, this anti-sex bias was to take an unusual turn. Since the difference between men and women was to be denied, women were held to be identical to men. That is not the same thing as saying that women were equal in dignity to men. By denying the physical differences between men and women, any distinction in gender-based roles was also destroyed. Men were not fathers and women were not mothers. Even beyond that, both men and women were merely spirits trapped in meaningless bodies. Since that was the case, in some limited corners of the Gnostic world women were ordained to the ministry. That is precisely the charge made against Marcion and why his own father excommunicated him.

It must be remembered that the Gnostics were just as persecuted as the early Christians. Therefore, they lacked uniformity and cohesion. What could be said about some of them could not be said of all. The ordination of women was not a widespread Gnostic reality. Possibly, ordination to the Gnostic diaconate was a bit more common. However, even this expression of the meaninglessness of the flesh with its embarrassing gender anomalies was localized in Syria and possibly Babylon. Gnostics simply were not allowed to develop anything close to a unified system.

As Christianity replaced paganism, the Gnostics lost much of their appeal. Gnostic elements did survive in Europe until the middle ages. Persecuted Bosnian Gnostics found shelter by accepting Islam during Turkish occupation. French Gnostics were eliminated during the Albigensian Crusade.

The Gnostic approach to the fundamental question of evil seems to have reappeared in our age. Natural religion, white witchcraft, and a tendency to obscure any differences based upon gender cast an uncomfortable Gnostic shadow. The old dual conclusions seem to spring from the same unlikely source. Since the physical differences between men and women are held in disdain, sex is unimportant and lacks moral value, except the equality of rights to indulge it. Celibacy and marital fidelity are of little value since both of these concepts get in the way of seeking anything, anytime, and anywhere. On the other hand, since gender-based roles are based on an unimportant set of physical accidents, men and women have no roles that can be denied to members of either gender. To be sure, society has justly recognized that members of either sex can perform most jobs. All human beings who offer their labor deserve the same just compensation for the same work. Only a few jobs appear to be gender specific, usually based upon strength and size.

However, things related to identity, more than to function, are not so easily ignored. The role of father may be dumped in the lap of a single mother. Likewise the role of mother may end up the responsibility of a father. Nevertheless, a mother or father has a specific identity, which can not be entirely assumed by one for the other. To deny in an absolute way that differences exist and mean something seems more in keeping with a Gnostic than a Christian worldview. Gnostics thought that every aspect of physical reality had to be warred against. Christians, even the more extreme Christians, believed that original creation had been good. It had been corrupted by man's sin, but what God made was good. The body was not evil. Sex may be the vehicle for passing on original sin but it was also the way of bringing new life to the world, and that was good. Christianity did not deny the differences between men and women. It recognized them as real.

Christianity does not get a pass on gender-based injustice. Women have been treated badly. They have never shared in the authority given to the Church. Longstanding injustices have to be addressed if the Church wants to continue in the direction set by Jesus.

At the same time, the differences between men and women are not to be completely ignored. They are as real as the male body of Jesus and the loving motherhood of Mary. Whole new ways of sharing authority may eventually take the place of ways which have long been accepted practice. In whatever way they evolve, they must include a respect for the created world. In the past that respect has resulted in a rejection of the Gnostic contempt for sexual differences between men and women. In Christ there may be no male or female, but that has never meant that the bodies of men and women have to be seen as identical. Nor has it meant that every role of one gender must be open to the other.

For two thousand years the living tradition of the Church has celebrated the differences between men and women in marriage and in ordination. Both have existed in every culture, age, and race where Christianity has taken root. Empires and kingdoms ruled by women and served by priestesses have hosted Christianity. In none of them has the universal Church obliterated the differences between men and women by either abolishing marriage or ordaining women to the priesthood. That is significant because the Church has sometimes been cut off from the seat of institutional authority in places where it adopted many of the elements of local culture without ever adopting an established female priesthood as an expression of local Christianity.

This poses a question that has to be considered. Since it was impossible to base the rejection of a female priesthood upon the oppressive authority of a male dominated institution in every isolated place on earth, why has tradition limited priesthood to males?

Easy answers are probably never going to be provable. Nevertheless, we are faced with the reality of time and space. In no place on this earth and at no time in human history has Christian tradition produced an ordained non-gender specific priesthood, at least not until the end of this millenium and in denominations not in union with either the Latin or Orthodox Churches.

We believe that Jesus Christ is contained in scripture and tradition. Both speak with one voice on this issue. Deaconesses are mentioned in the Acts of the Apostles and in early patristic writings. They were not ordained to that office nor did they function in the way that deacons functioned. One could, therefore, question their identity as part of an ordained hierarchy.

Is the choice to ordain only men to the priesthood another proclamation that the body is sacred and, male or female, it has significance? Is this sacramental reality, in fact, a rejection of the Gnostic concept of matter as evil or at least as insignificant? Does the male-only priesthood point to the uniqueness of each man and woman? Are the spiritual realities as real as the physical ones? Is it possible to reform authority without destroying sexual identity?

If the answer to all these questions results in the impossibility of ever ordaining women to the priesthood, what possible good can be accomplished by convincing large parts of the Church that the impossible may one day happen? If that is, indeed, an impossibility as tradition indicates, why promote alienation and bitterness based on this false hope? It is not unjust that I can not give birth to a child. It is reality. Perhaps, the same kind of spiritual realities have similar immutable consequences. Whatever those realities are, to the extent that they are human, they are sacred, have dignity, and shall be celebrated for all eternity.

All that being said, I am a man. More to the point, I am a white, middle-aged, celibate, ordained, Catholic, American male— the very definition of the oppressor in some circles. I have never felt the sting of discrimination based upon my gender. I also am a priest who loves his priesthood. I can not imagine being without it. I shall never know what it feels like to want something that sublime and not be able to have it. Conversely, because Jesus is a man and I am a heterosexual male, loving another man, even Jesus, might have elements easier for women to assimilate into their spiritual lives than for me. In any event, the whole discussion of defined gender roles has been tainted and is made infinitely more difficult because of the very real historical oppression of women. Is equality of dignity only possible if every physical part of a person's identity is completely and absolutely ignored? Christian Tradition, the pure and non-oppressive soul of it, suggests that the answer is, no.

Bones of Contention

BONE 11

Marriage

What God Has Joined,
Let No Man Divide

The most dangerous assumption anyone can make is that things have always been the way they are now. Such an assumption virtually guarantees that all subsequent decisions will rest on a faulty premise and fail to provide the support expected when they are most critically needed.

The minefield of commercial broadcasting is replete with tender ballads reminding the unsuspecting listener that men and women have fallen in love from the beginning and married. This has been true since Adam and Eve. It is touted as one of those immutable, bedrock conditions of humanity that will always be obvious to anyone. This theory is accepted universally and defended in the most credible arena available, the television talk show.

The only problem with this premise is that it is absolutely and completely wrong. Not only has romantic married love not been present in every historical age, it is not even the norm in many cultures at the present time. Polygamy is a respected institution in many parts of the world. There are even places where it is respectable to purchase a bride with a bag of sugar or an attractive goat. In many places arranged marriages between total strangers are still the norm. In some prosperous nations, men and women seldom dine, socialize, or communicate except in cases of absolute necessity.

I remember traveling in Morocco and suddenly coming to the realization that I had never seen a native Moroccan woman sitting on a chair in a public café. In fact, I seldom saw a woman in a café at all, and when I did she was always either a foreigner or sitting on the floor in an out of the way corner of the room. On my way to Azrule to purchase a handmade rug, I passed an old man holding the reins of a mule in his right hand and a stick in his left. An elderly woman was standing in front of the beast. She was looking down at the ground in a position of contrition. The mule was loaded with a substantial bundle of sticks, presumably firewood. The man was yelling at her in Arabic. Occasionally he struck her with the stick. It was not an especially strong blow. I think that its real sting was in its humiliation. I asked my Moroccan driver to explain what my Western eyes had just beheld. He informed me that the man was shouting insults at his wife because she was *wearing out the mule*. Since, presumably, the mule was more valuable than the wife was, she should have placed the bundle of sticks on her own back and spared the beast for more valuable service.

This would not be the only challenge to what I had come to take for granted concerning the universal character of marriage. Upon arriving at Azrule, I discovered an American orphanage. Baptist missionaries from Oklahoma operated it. In the interior of Morocco I found Arab and Berber children who spoke perfect English, but with a southwestern Oklahoma accent. One of the children immediately adopted me as the father she had never had. She had never seen a Catholic priest and had no idea that anyone on this planet ever took a vow not to marry. She naturally assumed that I had a family. She asked if she could correspond with me and call me *daddy*. I didn't see any harm.

For the next few years I got letters and cards addressing me as *dearest daddy*. That was cute until Lisa reached seventeen years of age. She became increasingly attractive, and I became increasingly uncomfortable having photos laying around the rectory that had "To my dearest daddy" written on the back.

In her last letter to me Lisa described the man she was soon to marry. She spoke about him in the usual glowing, teenage terms. He was *wonderful, strong, handsome, kind,* and, of course, *loving.* Lisa mentioned that he seldom beat her. That was her description of Mr. Wonderful. I immediately wrote back, expressing my disapproval of any man who would beat the woman he claimed to love. That was my last communication with Lisa. I never got another letter from her and all future letters from me were returned. The head of the orphanage finally wrote to me notifying me that Lisa had married and moved away from Azrule. He knew of no way that I could find her.

Sadly, I think that for most people in the world, Lisa's marriage has more in common with the norm than that of my parents, who seemed to draw such strength from their love for each other. Knowing what I do concerning spousal abuse in our own country, I hardly feel any kind of smug cultural ascendancy. At least other cultures are more up front and honest when they treat women like some kind of grudged necessity. Nevertheless, the worldwide struggle to protect the human dignity of women seems to be more of a Western phenomenon. One might even make the claim that it is really only politically effective in countries that are wealthy, industrialized and Christian.

In the West equality of pay, reproductive issues, and employment practices are of primary concern. In most other parts of the world, survival is the main issue. It might be wrong to focus on the extremes, but they do exist. Murdered and abused wives are part of the American cultural landscape just as much as starving veiled widows with no man to lead them out of the house to purchase food are part of the Afghan reality. How is Christianity to address this situation, and what is the historical context for its actions?

In the Roman Empire of the first century marriage took as many forms as there were peoples within the empire. However, some things were common nearly everywhere. Marriage was a private matter. There were no set ceremonies or legal procedures. The majority of people, at least of those living in the city of Rome, were not free citizens, and therefore were not even allowed to marry. Those individuals who could marry avoided the institution as long as they could. Marriage was so unattractive that a number of emperors issued laws requiring it for all young men. Making marriage a matter of coercion spoke volumes about its unattractiveness to many people.

People married for a number of reasons. First, among these was because they had to. It was the law. However, they also married out of civic duty. Marriage was the only way of producing future free citizens for the empire. Well-connected marriages were also ways of promoting family prosperity and prominence. Marriage was also a way of keeping family lands in the family. Heirs were of immense value to any man.

There were also certain handicaps. Even pagan married men were expected to be faithful to their wives. In a society with plenty of female slaves and few sexual mores for the rest of society, marriage put a severe limit on a young man's sex life.

It was difficult to know who was, in fact, married. With no documents to establish it and no public ceremony to celebrate it, and with few social events attended by husband and wife to showcase it, the only people who really knew for sure that a couple was married was the couple. When things got boring, either party was allowed to end the marriage with a divorce. If there had been a dowry, it was returned to the wife's family. All children were usually left with the husband. The wife had no rights as far as her children were concerned. There is little evidence that many divorcing women wanted any.

Despite the anything-goes mentality of most Roman citizens, when it came to sex between husbands and wives it was difficult to see much difference between rape and conjugal union. Following the *wedding night,* a new bride was often presented to a drunken assembly of the groom's friends as the *shamed* bride. She, for her part, had waited in terror the night before, dreading her husband's entry into her bedchamber, who then ravished her with absolute non-concern for her needs or emotional state.

To be sure, the marriages of some men and women did eventually grow into love. However, they were real exceptions and spoken of in terms of extraordinary virtue. A really good man was kind to his slaves, gentle with his horse, and loved his wife. None of these things were thought of as a necessity. However they were virtuous.

There was one group in the Empire that did not quite fit the usual mold, Jews. In direct contrast to the unregulated private pagan model, Judaism honored marriage as the ideal human state established by God at the time of creation. It was a basic human institution protected and highly regulated by law. Jewish marriages were public celebrations. Even the period of betrothal was a community event. Few pagans could be sure of a neighbor's marital status, but there was no ambiguity when it came to Jewish marriage.

Unlike the nations around them, there was little tolerance for any form of incest. Thus, the Jewish family avoided inbreeding and family isolation. It was necessary to constantly invite new and complex relationships to be established between families. This, along with a proscription against marrying non-Jews, provided social cohesion within the community.

If pagans could be said to marry as a matter of civic duty, Jews could be said to marry out of religious conviction and family loyalty. Of course, celibacy was not unknown to first century Jews. It was a high ideal in the Essene community. However, it was neither common nor easy to reconcile with the normative Jewish view.

Jewish husbands had ten obligations toward their wives and four rights in respect to them. The husband was required to provide his wife with sustenance and maintenance; clothing and lodging; to cohabit with her; to provide a fixed allowance for her; to procure medical attention and care; to provide for her support in the event of his death; and to provide a just portion of his estate for her male children. The husband received the benefit of his wife's handiwork; was entitled to her chance gains or finds; had the use of her property; and had the right to inherit her estate.

The point of the legal cocoon of legal protection was the establishment of peace and harmony within the family. However, the legal proscriptions did not require a husband to treat his wife with equality or even seek her advice on anything. Girls and women were not compelled to study or become learned. Men and women were simply responsible for different aspects of life. Men held the primacy of authority in the family. They were expected, more than required, to treat wives with affection and tenderness. Only men could request a divorce. However, a wife could force her husband to do so in certain limited circumstances.

The lack of social interaction between husbands and wives is reflected in the Christian Gospels. Jesus was lost in the temple because men and women did not normally travel in the same company. As a child, Jesus could have been with either the men or the women. Thus, his loss was not immediately obvious to either Mary or Joseph until the men and women came together for rest and water.

Nevertheless, compared to pagan marriage, Jewish marriage was infinitely more stable and noble. Springing from this tradition, Christianity was to infuse greater respect for marriage into the nations of the Empire.

Perhaps the greatest revolutionary result of the ascendancy of Christianity, after the belief in the resurrection, was the recognition of the human dignity of women. Since circumcision was not the backbone of Christian initiation, men and women were brought into the community in exactly the same way. Baptized women were no longer disposable resources. Even Judaism had allowed men to dispose of wives if they could be shown to be rebellious or *disgusting*. Jesus admonished against discarding women through divorce for any reason, *lewd conduct being a separate case.*

St. Paul might demand that women not speak in church, but he also wrote that in Christ there was no male or female. Far from suggesting the overthrow of the existing social order, Paul accepted a subservient role for women, which at the same time insisted upon the recognition of their spiritual dignity. He seemed to establish a kind of concept of separate but spiritually equal roles for women and men. A husband was the head of the family. The wife was expected to obey him. Nevertheless, he was obligated to love her as if she were his own body, another concept borrowed from Judaism, and one that was not optional.

What has all this to do with life at the beginning of the new millenium? It is the context in which Christian marriage was first defined and presented. Christian marriage was a continuation of the revolutionary Jewish concept that women and relationships with women were sacred. In this context romantic love between a husband and wife was a Christian development of the importance of women. Polygamy and remarriage after divorce were not possible because the bond between a man and woman was important.

The evolution of marriage away from a private pagan institution to a sacramental presence of Jesus continues to this day. Jesus set the direction. Human love is to be protected, nourished, and reverenced. God, who is love, is present in married love. The Talmud says that where two or three are gathered to study the Torah, the Shekhina is among them. Jesus says something similar about two or three gathered in His name. The Talmud goes on to say that the Shekhina is also present in the love between a worthy husband and wife. The Catholic Church continues this development by maintaining that marriage is a sacrament, a unique real presence of Jesus Christ on earth.

People can not have it both ways. Either marriage is sacred with incredible dignity and is an act of God, or it is merely a human act that can be erased. If sacramental marriage is holy and an act of God, it can not be destroyed. Of necessity this means that frail human beings are occasionally going to be unable to live up to its demands.

It is difficult for me to see people in pain. I listen to people who come to me saying that they do not really believe that they ever were married in the eyes of God. They may have walked down the aisle of a Catholic Church and recited vows in the presence of a priest. They may have lived together for years and produced a number of children. Yet at least one of them can still come forward and claim that he or she was forced into marriage, or didn't know what marriage was, or perhaps, was simply unable to love the other person in the way they had vowed. As a representative of the Church, I listen and do all that I am able to bring peace to tormented people.

It is painful to want to get on with your life after a long and bitter period of contention. However, I have also discovered that it is painful to be the abandoned wife who did not want the divorce, who believes in living the vows she has made even when she is abandoned and left behind. It is painful for a husband to see his wife newly married in the Catholic Church—when he feels like he is the injured party and the Church he loves has just given its blessing to his wife's adultery. But what else can the Church do but listen and allow the parties to make their best case?

Most of the annulments granted in the world are given to American Catholics. People in every other nation, including very poor third world countries, seem to understand very clearly what marriage is and how to validly enter into one. In our technologically advanced nation, Catholic people are so lacking in the basic understanding of what marriage is that an annulment is likely to be granted to anyone who applies for it. There are many reasons for this tragic situation. In general Americans never expect to be held accountable for any decisions they make. There must always be a second chance, an alibi round, a fine to pay that makes it possible to forget the past and to get on with life. It seems unfair and un-American for anyone to be expected to keep his word for the rest of his life.

Yet compassion does play a part. What would Jesus do? The Church does its best to answer that question in concrete ways every day. It is in a *no-win* situation. If it says no to annulments, it looks harsh and unforgiving. If it allows them, then it looks hypocritical and sometimes is perceived as unfair to the injured party. The balancing act between its human and its divine nature is played out in the Church's ministry to the divorced and broken-hearted. No matter what the Church does it will be attacked and berated.

Mary Lee was a self-made Catholic. She lived in a rural part of Missouri quite a distance from any Catholic Church. She had arranged to take a correspondence course on the Catholic faith and had come to believe all that the Church teaches. She then taught her children what she had found and invited them to request baptism along with her. One daughter had opted not to become Catholic. Both of her sons were baptized into the Church with her.

One evening Marry Lee called to ask a special favor of me. Her great-aunt was near death. She wanted to see a priest, but was not sure one would come. The aunt had lived for more than seventy years with a husband she had married outside of the Catholic Church. She had been baptized but had received no other sacraments and had not been to mass during her married life. I called the local pastor and asked him for permission to see this woman.

She was coming to the end of a long and painful cancer. There was not a lot left of her. She seemed like a living skeleton. I could have easily picked her up with one arm. I asked her if she would like to make her peace with God. She said, "Yes." I asked her family to give me a moment alone with her. She then made her first confession. I called the family back into the room. I anointed her, then as an after thought, I confirmed her. She received her first communion after a short preparation. Then I asked her if she would like me to bless her marriage.

She said, "Oh, please."

Her husband was glad to accommodate her request.

I invited them to join hands. She was beginning to fail.

I asked her husband, "Do you take this woman to be your wife? Will you promise to be true to her in good times and in bad, in sickness and in health? Will you love her and honor her all the days of her life?"

He said, "Yes."

When I asked the great-aunt the same question she had already lost the ability to speak.

I took her by the hand and said, "If the answer is, 'yes,' just squeeze my hand."

I felt her faintly tighten her grip on my hand. I continued, "You have declared your intention to enter into marriage before God and His Church. Therefore, what God has joined together let no man divide."

I asked the ninety-two-year-old groom if the bride he first took more than seventy years earlier still looked good to him after all those years.

He said, "She's beautiful."

He kissed his bride on the cheek. A single little tear rolled down from the corner of her eye.

That night his bride went to heaven.

As I left that house, I remember thinking to myself, "Surely, this is what Jesus meant when he spoke about marriage."

Bones of Contention

BONE 12

Abortion

The Gift

My mother had gone to the hospital. Dad said that she wasn't really sick, but the hospital seemed like a strange place for my mom to go if she were well.

I was in the first grade at St. Ann's school. It was three o'clock and time to go home. Everyone else cleared out as soon as Sister signaled that we were dismissed. I was left alone, waiting for my dad.

I loved my teacher like a second mother. In some small way, I think that she knew that and returned it. She noticed that I was standing on the sidewalk in front of the school—a little lost soul. Sister invited me to the convent.

I don't know if I was afraid or just overwhelmed! I had never imagined that I would ever see the inside of the convent. I would have been more comfortable being invited into the Oval Office. However, Sister knew the way to my heart. Milk and cookies were all I needed to calm down and feel at home.

Dad arrived a few minutes later, with the news that I had a brother! Exactly how this wonderful event had taken place, I could not say. I knew that my mother was getting really big. She told me that I would soon be getting a new sister or brother. That had been our private secret, until mom and dad gave me permission to tell my aunts and uncles at a family gathering. Then, all of a sudden, I went from the important person with special news to an invisible speck, while all the women laughed and hugged my mom. The whole affair seemed somehow out of balance, since I was obviously no longer the center of it.

I went to school as usual and ended the day as a big brother. The new kid was named Steve. He looked a lot like a pink catfish. That yellow stuff in his diaper was more than I could handle, but mom didn't seem to mind it all that much. People kept reminding me that I was more important now that I was a big brother, but I remember feeling a lot less special now that there were two of us.

If I had to have a brother, Steve was about the best I could hope for. Even as a baby, he was an independent little kid. He didn't make a lot of noise, and I still ruled the roost, at least for a few more years.

When my mom told us that we would soon have another brother, things seemed different. Mom was coughing more and was always tired. She went to the doctor more this time than when she was carrying Steve. The whole family was happy, but I could also tell that everyone was worried. Something was wrong.

One horrible night mom got sick. Dad called the neighbor ladies in to help. They dressed mom to take her to the hospital. It was far too early for us to get a new brother. Mom was in pain and crying. Everyone was in a hurry. I started to cry. To quiet me down, dad let me take my pet dog into bed with me. I had actually managed to sneak my dog into my room before that night, but this was the first authorized dog sleep-over. I knew things had to be serious.

Mom was gone for several weeks. In those days, children were not allowed to visit patients in the hospital. Dad took me to the hospital every day, and I waved to mom as she looked down from her window. She had to be at least ten stories above me, but seeing her wave back gave me the reassurance I needed.

Dad did not talk about the new baby or about how sick mom was. One morning he told me that I was going to be allowed to go up to mom's room with him. He didn't show any emotion, and that frightened me.

When I entered mom's room, she was sitting up in bed and looked really good. She asked me how I had been getting along without her. I lied and said that I was doing all right. We both knew that I was not telling the truth. I hugged her for a long time. Neither of us said anything.

Then mom told me to sit on the edge of her bed, so we could talk. I didn't like that. Dad had already told me that it was against the rules for me to sit on mom's bed. If she was breaking the rules, things had to be bad.

Mom told me that her heart and lungs were sick. Her lungs were full of phlegm, and the doctor didn't think that mom's heart was strong enough to keep both her and her baby alive. Mom explained that the doctor wanted to have the baby come now, but that would mean that the baby would probably not be strong enough to live. If mom kept the baby inside of her, she might not live. I was there so that mom could tell me good-bye.

I really couldn't understand a lot of what she said. Dad said nothing at all. For the first time in his life, he seemed empty and helpless. Mom told me that she could not live if it meant that her baby had to die. She told me that some day I would understand. She wanted me to know that she loved me very much. If she did not get well and come home, it was not because I had been a bad boy, or that she wanted to go away. She hugged me good-bye. It would take years before I fully realized what had taken place.

My mother was very sick for a very long time. Her baby was born several weeks early. For a time it looked as if he would not live, but, eventually, both mom and my newest brother came home. My brother, David, was a lot louder than Steve had been. Actually, he didn't look that bad. He had been taken from mom and had not endured the trauma of natural birth. He looked healthy, but he had a few rough years ahead. Mom never really recovered.

The medical bills took nearly everything my parents had. We almost lost our house. It was only a four-room, frame home, one of those instant tract houses built for returning World War II veterans and their families. To my folks it was everything, and they were terrified of losing it.

Dad took an extra, part-time job. He already worked forty hours each week at Wagner Electric. Now, he pumped gas at a local service station until late at night. On weekends he collected garbage. He still could not earn enough money to pay the bills. For the family to survive, dad had to take out an illegal third mortgage on the house.

It all seemed about to come crashing down. I do not know how many nights my mom and dad sat at the kitchen table trying to make the money cover all the bills. Mom sometimes cried; dad just looked hollow eyed.

Food became simpler, fatter, and starchy. Homemade noodles, biscuits, gravy, navy beans, and scrambled eggs were about all we ate. Finally, mom had to take a job.

I don't know whom it hurt more for mom to work, dad or me. I hated coming home to an empty house, but dad really seemed defeated. Mom did not work because she wanted to, or because she had nothing to do at home. She was needed at home. The new baby was sickly. Steve was not yet in school, and I felt alone.

Her job did not pay very much. She worked in a factory, but women were paid less than men for the same work. The factory was unheated in the winter and unventilated in the summer. It was a horrible place. One Saturday mom had to work overtime. Dad took me to visit mom at work. I hated seeing my mother in that dirty place. Dad tried to keep his feelings to himself, but I could see the hurt in his eyes.

Through it all, our folks kept us in the Catholic school. I do not know how they managed to do it, but no thought was ever given to sending us to the public school. I think of that often when I hear anyone refer to Catholic schools as *schools for the rich*. The joke was that we were really rich, but it had nothing to do with money.

The doctor had proposed inducing labor for my brother. It would have not exactly been an abortion. In those days, that would have been illegal. Nevertheless, a delivery that early would have surely meant the death of the child. Mom would not consent to any procedure that would save her life at such a cost.

I am pro life. Nevertheless, I have great sympathy for women and girls who are faced with that kind of decision. I cannot sit in judgement on women facing such terror. I believe that, in every case, abortion is absolutely wrong. Still, I recognize the fear and pain that many women endure. I pray that they will have the courage that I admired so much in my mom.

My mother was ready to die for the love of a child she had yet to hold. That meant that she would have given her life for any of her children—Steve, David, or me. Our mother loved us more than she wanted to live. That's not theory; that's fact. We all carried that knowledge with us every moment of our lives.

It was the day before Christmas. A few years earlier dad had died. Mom was not doing well. Steve was sitting beside her hospital bed. Mom was in a coma. David had just joined us. None of us said anything. I finally broke the silence; "I would like to give mom the sacrament of the anointing of the sick." There was a lump in my throat. It was difficult to speak. I put the oil of the sick on her forehead. I paused for just a moment. I was in that same hospital that I had been in thirty years earlier, when mom had said good-bye. I had no way of repaying her for her life and love, but Jesus could.

The words came out; "Through this holy anointing may the Lord in His love and mercy help you with the grace of the Holy Spirit. May the Lord who frees you from sin save you and raise you up." That day she was with Him in Paradise.

She had lived fifty-two years, the same number of years that God had given to dad. They both had been part of the great generation. Neither of them had gone to school past the eighth grade, but all of their children had college degrees. They had outlived a depression, world war, segregation, and witnessed men walking on the moon. They chose the Catholic faith for their family at a time of revolutionary renewal. They wanted stability and security for their children, but adapted heroically to social upheaval.

They invented ways to protect the dignity of their children that could only have been the result of genius. Since we were truly poor, mom insisted that I wear a clean, starched, white shirt to school every day. During the really lean years, she gave me a dime to carry in my pocket. She told me that I should never spend it, but if anyone said that I was poor, I was to show them my dime, and tell them that I had money, but I didn't want to spend it. I still have that dime.

There is not a single day that I do not think of my folks and miss them. However, one day is very special for my youngest brother. On that day he celebrates the gift he was given. Every January, on the anniversary of Roe v. Wade, David, now an ordained deacon, marches for life in Washington, D.C. Mom is with him.

BONE 13

Ecumenism

I am of Paul;
I am of Apolos;
I am of Cephas

Another October had come to Apple Creek. The sugar maples in front of the rectory were more magnificent than they had been in previous years. The parish owls had once again hatched their young in the hollow part of the tree in front of the church. They were nearly grown and had begun hunting on their own. My three gray geese, Moe, Larry, and Curly, had also come to full maturity and were beginning to make themselves a nuisance to the parishioners.

One morning I saw them swimming in the plastic wading pool that I had bought for them. They began to go faster and faster in the little pool. Finally, they began fighting one another. Their beautiful long necks were all tangled together. They were biting each other. Curly was bloody from the fight.

I immediately went down to make peace. I gently untangled their necks, speaking softly to them as I separated them. Then I continued speaking to them with tender sounding words. My three geese looked at each other with their beautiful blue eyes. Then they looked at me, the peacemaker. Then they began to bite and chase me. That's when I knew that my geese were Catholic members of the parish.

I had a special friend. That spring, a wounded wild turkey had made his way to my back porch and had begun roosting in the safety of the house. He had probably fought an egg-stealing raccoon to a draw and barely survived. I named him Thomas Aquinas— not all that original for a male turkey.

He seemed grateful for the sanctuary and had actually become completely tame, at least to me. Every morning he waited near the back door. I never locked the doors of the rectory. I didn't even close the inside door. So Thomas could look through the glass and see me coming down from my bedroom. If I did not throw him a piece of bread or some other treat, he made an awful fuss. He'd gobble and strut and peck at the glass until I came out and either fed him or scratched him on the chest. Sometimes I actually had to pick him up before he would calm down.

Thomas was my protector. That was cute until he decided that people should stay away from me. Often he would strut up and down the front sidewalk, chasing anyone who dared to approach my door. It was time for Thomas to move on.

The sweet smell of burning wood was in the air. This was apple butter weekend. The men of the parish had been manning the copper kettles all night, while the women worked in the parish kitchen cooking food and preparing the jars for the apple butter. Making apple butter was a real community event. It was one of the last tasks that brought the people together to share the harvest and the work. In earlier days, there had been many such occasions. Farmers used to share machinery. They needed all the help they could get to bring in the crops and prepare for the winter. Few were wealthy enough to own a large machine for just their own farm. In the past, they had gathered to bail hay and straw, to harvest wheat and corn, to butcher, to plant, to build, and to dig wells. However, these days, there were enough machines for a single farmer to do most of those things by himself. Farmers needed each other less, except for making apple butter.

The women and children worked all day peeling, coring, and cutting up the apples. The men stayed up all night continually stirring the apples and keeping the fires burning under the kettles. They always brought samples of this year's new homemade wine to share with their neighbors. The women always complained to the priest about how much the men shared.

Once again, I was called upon to give the annual lecture to the men concerning their drinking. At the end of my usual sermon, one of the guilty parties sheepishly offered me a drink of his best vintage. I, as usual, sampled his bottle, and then I heard one of the women mutter, "He's just like the rest of them!" and the women all went back to work in the kitchen.

I doubt that the women ever really expected me to break up the party. In fact, I think that they rather expected me to first chastise the men, and then join them. They complained because it was part of the script. Every part of this little morality play had been written generations before I had ever been assigned to Apple Creek.

There would be a new custom beginning this year. Since the time of Andrew Jackson, whose name appeared on the parish land grant, the community had been divided almost in half. The farmers living west of highway 61 were Catholic. Those living east of the highway were Missouri Synod Lutherans. The Catholics were Bavarians; the Lutherans were Saxons.

Until quite recently, they had not mixed much. However, God, in His infinite wisdom, had made that a necessity. For some unexplainable reason, most of the children born to the Catholic community were boys, while the Lutherans had an unusually large crop of girls. Religion was still more important than nature, but nature ran a close second. Mixed marriages had become commonplace.

It was time to begin building bridges. That was obvious to anyone who attended a baptism. Whether the child of a mixed marriage was baptized in the Catholic Church or the Lutheran Church, the scenario was always the same—a set of grandparents with tears in their eyes. When I baptized a child of mixed parents, I always shortened the litany of the saints to be as inoffensive to the Lutheran grandparents as possible. I also made it a policy to invite the people to pray the Protestant version of the Lord's Prayer on such occasions. I usually acknowledged the pain of the broken-hearted grandparents and reminded everyone that the Catholic side had won nothing by seeing such profound sorrow. It was past time to mend the hurt.

My suggestion to invite all of our Lutheran neighbors to a free Reformation Day breakfast was met with uncharacteristic enthusiasm. Most of my German parishioners did not usually express such open support of anything. They were the best poker players in the state. But this idea really stirred them up.

No one knew whether or not our neighbors would accept our invitation. Most of the Catholics had never set foot on Lutheran holy ground. Most of the Lutherans had never been to our parish. Even though we had all long ago learned how to live as good neighbors and many of our families were now joined by mixed marriages, there were still invisible boundaries which both sides were careful to observe.

The word reached us on apple butter weekend that our neighbors had accepted our offer. No one at Apple Creek talked about anything else. Old stories were shared at the fire in between pulls on the wine jug. Some of the old men laughed about walking to school on the Catholic side of the highway, trading insults with the Lutheran kids on the Lutheran side of the road. Lutheran children threw rocks at *Catholic* pigs. The Catholics reciprocated by stinging *Lutheran* dairy cattle with rocks. Now, old friends, they were to gather for the first time in one spot at one of the beloved and dreaded churches.

All week the children in St. Joseph's School made signs and banners to welcome our neighbors to the First Annual Reformation Day Breakfast, sponsored by St. Joseph's Catholic Church. The signs were touching and childlike. *God Bless You on Your Special Day,* and *May God Watch Over Our Good Neighbors* were two that seemed to sum up the enthusiasm on our side.

Before the day even began, the people of St. Joseph's of Apple Creek had donated every mouthful of food that would be served to our neighbors. Flats of fresh eggs and prized home-smoked bacon and sausage were contributed. Our parish women made their best coffeecake. All morning the smell of fresh bread surrounded the parish like incense. Everything was ready, but would our neighbors really come?

There had never been an event at Apple Creek that had greater participation. All of the women cooked. The men parked cars, and a few took it upon themselves to be official greeters. The young people waited on tables and picked up dirty dishes. Yes, our neighbors came, many with tears in their eyes, this time of gratitude and joy.

They were still German. They didn't want to take handouts from anyone. Many demanded to at least pay something for the breakfast. Their money was refused, but the Lutheran men took up a collection among themselves, and left it in a coffee can on the counter. It was found after they all had gone home. By noon of that day, more than five hundred guests had been counted. Everyone was exhausted, but so very proud and happy. We had the honor of making the first step.

In the days that followed, many of the people of the parish had some explaining to do. Catholic neighbors in surrounding parishes wanted to know what Apple Creek was doing, *celebrating* Reformation Sunday! The people knew how to answer such complaints. They were just being Catholic. They had served their neighbors at table with respect and dignity. The Catholic people of Apple Creek had not insulted their neighbors or acted triumphal, nor did they back off from what they believed Christianity to be all about. If Catholics had responded to their neighbors in this way five hundred years earlier, perhaps the division which caused so much pain would have never taken place.

On the day that marks the shattering of Christianity, Catholic farmers served their Lutheran neighbors by feeding them and waiting on them. Old friends were honored. Prayers were offered for them. The things they held most sacred were respected. That was what it meant for the people of Apple Creek to be Catholic.

The following summer, our Lutheran neighbors responded by having a Catholic appreciation kettle beef dinner. The Lutheran ladies had heard rumors, totally true, that the priest at Apple Creek had publicly announced that, while the Catholics made the best chicken and dumplings in Perry County, the Lutherans made the best coffeecake. All the Catholic ladies agreed.

When I got to the Lutheran hall for our special dinner, the ladies had a closet, all shelved off, full of coffeecake. They proudly insisted that I try several of their best. Then a doggie bag was packed for me to take home.

Shortly after our third annual Reformation Day breakfast, I got the news that I had been transferred to another parish. Following the wonderful going away party at Apple Creek, I was invited to stop by the Lutheran hall in Uniontown. Our neighbors were having one of their fund raising dinners. They had stretched a banner over highway 61. It read, "Farewell to *Our* Father John." When I think of that, I still tear up.

It is still not possible for Lutherans and Catholics of Perry County to pray together, at least not officially. The leaders of our Churches have some things to settle before we are allowed that joy. Perhaps in the long run we accomplished very little, but we did build a bridge. It was only a footbridge, not big enough for the traffic it needs to carry. Future generations may laugh at the modest things we were able to accomplish, and not think of them as accomplishments at all. However, in the back of my mind, I can not help believing that real healing takes place in just this way. A lot of bitterness and fear died on a plate of scrambled eggs. We did what we could do. We poured the foundation. What others may build on it will be a wonder to see.

BONE 14

Faith

Hanging in the Dark

I left the Marine Corps in 1974. My early attempts at testing my vocation became an exercise in removing the acquired rough edges that I had cultivated in the service. Along with my verbal and social transformation, my body underwent a significant metamorphosis. I had gained a nice protective layer of adipose tissue around my middle. Most folks just call it *middle age spread*. Whatever I called it, it was the result of doing less and eating more.

In the four years I was in the seminary, I had never entered the old gymnasium. It was in general disrepair. The seminary had at one time been bursting at the seams with young men eager to become priests. In my time it was no more than half full, and one of the two gyms was no longer in use. It was actually in the basement of the east wing.

I loved theology. Using my mind to ferret out obscure points of dogma was wonderful after several years of relative mental and religious inactivity. I could hardly be kept busy enough. I applied for the Master of Arts program at the seminary. That meant a little extra work. I still had time on my hands.

The academic dean gave me permission to simultaneously peruse a masters' degree in European History at the local state university. On top of all that, I turned my field education assignment at a local home for troubled boys into a forty-hour a week job. With the prayer schedule at the seminary, I kept comfortably busy.

From time to time every institution tightens up its discipline. The formation team decided that we were staying out too late and spending less time at the seminary. Father Dan announced that from that night on, the doors of the seminary would be locked at midnight. Anyone who returned after that hour would have to ring the bell at the front door waking up everyone in the seminary, students and faculty. The only problem was that I got off work at midnight, and had to race across town to get back as close as possible to midnight.

At first, things went well. Father Dan was not as rigid as he pretended to be. *Midnight* usually meant twelve or twelve thirty-ish. For several weeks I made it back to find the doors unlocked; everything was fine. Then, on the coldest day of the winter, disaster befell me. I got home to find the doors locked tight. Most lights were out. I tried to rouse some of my friends to come and let me in, but no one came to my rescue. I was faced with either driving to my mother's home to spend the night or finding a more creative way to get into the building. It was cold. Spending the night in my car was out of the question.

That old basement gym was located just to the left of the side door. I noticed that it had a broken window at ground level. It only took a few minutes to decide to give it a try.

It was a tight fit, but I was soon through the window, hanging from the center part of the frame. I suddenly realized that I had not really thought the situation through. I was hanging in the dark without knowing how far a drop it was to the floor. I also did not know what might be under me. My mind made full use of its powers of imagination and creativity. Would I land on a pile of free weights and break an ankle? Would a volleyball pole, sticking straight up…? That was too awful to consider.

I decided to pull myself up and go to my mother's house. However, by that time, I had hung a bit too long, and my arms were too tired to pull me back up. I hung a bit longer and then began yelling for help. It was no use. This end of the building was almost totally deserted at that time of night.

My arms ached. I was forming bruises and sores on my forearms. I could feel my grip beginning to loosen. Very soon I would drop to an unknown fate. I held on as long as possible.

Finally, my hands just let go. It was not a conscious choice on my part. I simply fell—about three inches!

All that had been necessary was for me to stretch out my toes, and I would have felt the floor, inches beneath me. I have seldom felt so silly. At that moment I was glad that I had failed to rouse help. I could only guess at the entertainment value that I would have given my friends, if they had come to rescue me and found me clinging to life inches above the floor. Once again God had protected my dignity.

The next day, I was grateful to wear my cassock. It covered my arms. I kept the drama of the previous night to myself. Upon request, Father Dan gave me the combination code to the new punch-in lock for the side door. I was never placed in that position again.

After a few weeks to put the whole affair behind me, I began to see how many times I had been saved from myself in just that way. Hindsight is a wonderful tool for spiritual discernment. Going into situations, I had often been unable to discover the will of God. Looking back, it always seemed obvious.

Often, my response to God has been similar to my dilemma. When I have been too afraid to turn loose and let God catch me, He sometimes has let me hang until I simply had no choice. When I did eventually fall, I almost always have been surprised at how short a fall it was and how gently God caught me.

I know that having faith is sometimes very difficult. My mind has accepted that God will always be there for me, but many times I am still afraid to let go. I wish I could root that fear entirely out of my life. Unfortunately, I have been only slightly successful in learning how to fall into the dark with trust and courage.

I once asked a valued, retired, priest friend when I could expect to finally have enough faith, to let God have complete control of my life. He was in his late eighties and was the most spiritually mature man I had ever known. I still find his answer one of the most profound challenges I have to face in my daily life.

When does a person learn how to trust God completely?

He said. "John, you'll have to ask someone older and holier than me."

I have yet to find that person.

Resurrection

An Easter Morning Story

Some ideas are so profound that they can only be expressed in parables and understood by children or, in very rare cases, adults who have the ability to be childlike. *The Resurrection* is one of these sublime realities. My friend, Fr. Bob Porter, told this little story to me. It was originally used as a Good Friday story. It ended in death. I have added a little to make it an explanation of the Easter miracle.

There once lived a funny looking little man and his simple little wife. They had a small cottage outside of town and kept mostly to themselves.

The little man earned what money they needed by operating the Railroad Bridge over the river near their home. He and his wife didn't need much to get by. They were about as happy as two poor people could be, except for one thing. They desperately wanted a child.

As the years passed they almost abandoned their hope of ever being a family. Then, finally, when it seemed most unlikely, they had a son!

Now their joy was complete! The simple little woman and the funny looking man could not have given their child more love. Everything he did amazed them. They were proud of their son and he was proud of them. There had never been a more perfectly complete family.

Life for them had a comfortable rhythm. Every day mama would make lunch for her husband. She lovingly packed his plain meal in a pail. The child had a similar, but smaller, can. When his papa left for work, the little one trailed behind him imitating his daddy's big steps.

Every morning father and son set off for the railroad bridge. They ate their lunch together, and then the father threw the switch that opened the bridge allowing the train to pass. Then he closed the bridge so that the boats on the river could navigate the channel, while the little one played nearby.

One day the father and son got to the bridge a little early. It was an especially beautiful day. The little man sat down under a tree and soon fell asleep. The boy chased butterflies and picked wildflowers like he usually did. As his papa slept, the child worked his way down to the river's edge. He lay on the cement slab where the bridge would rest after his father threw the switch. The little guy was mesmerized by the river. He threw some of his dandelions into the passing water and watched them disappear. Then he fell asleep, just like his father.

After a while, his papa awoke to the whistle of an approaching train. He looked around for his little boy. To his horror he saw his child lying right where the huge railroad bridge would come to rest.

He frantically called to his son. But the little one was far away and so soundly asleep that he could not hear his father.

The father was near panic! He had to throw the switch. If he did not, all those people would die, and they were counting on him. But if he did, he would crush his only son to death—his son who meant everything to him.

The little man hesitated for only a moment. He knew what he had to do. Blinded by tears, he threw the switch. The huge, iron bridge came down and crushed his only son to death.

As the train passed safely over the bridge some of the first class passengers noticed the funny looking little man slumped over the switch. They could not see that he was crying. Some of them laughed at him. But most hardly noticed him at all.

After the train had passed and the bridge had been returned to its original position, the little man climbed down the bank and gathered up the broken body of his little boy. He wrapped all that was left of his son in his worn old over-coat and held him in his arms, rocking him and gently speaking to him with tender, loving words. All night the little man held the body of his son. By early morning, he knew that his wife would be beside herself, worrying about where he and their child were. He began the painful walk home, carrying the body of his boy.

Halfway home he met his wife.

"What's wrong?" she asked almost begging to hear the response she wanted to hear.

But the little man could not speak. He just unwrapped the face of their child and held him up so that his mother could see him.

She didn't scream as he expected. She was calm and quiet. This confused the little man. He looked down expecting to see the lifeless face of his only son, but he did not see what he knew he would see. Instead, the little one had his sparkling eyes open. The child smiled a big warm, loving smile. Then the little boy reached up with his tiny hand and wiped his father's tears away and said: **"Oh, papa, didn't you know that anyone who loves like you can never really taste death?"**

The Son is alive! And anyone who loves like His Father loves shall never really taste death.

Christ is risen!

Indeed! He is risen!

Bones of Contention

BONE 16

Liturgical Music

Sing a New Song

I believe that I was in eighth grade. Sister Mary Celeste took our class over to the parish Church for music practice. She began by explaining that since the Second Vatican Council called for the mass to be prayed in the language of the people, it was important to learn new songs that everyone could understand. No more *Ave Maria* or *Tantum Ergo,* from now on we would be singing songs that we could understand. The first of these would be introduced at tomorrow's school mass. It would replace the meaningless medieval music of the dusty past. We opened our new songbooks to the first of many new and more meaningful songs, *Kum-by-ya.* Sister did not know what Kum-by-ya meant. She guessed that it meant something like, "Come by here," but she didn't know for sure. Yep! Songs that were meaningful—but no one could tell us what they meant. That was my introduction to liturgical reform.

It is called *cognitive dissonance.* It is the ability to say or sing things that either mean absolutely nothing at all or that are diametrically opposed to one's most cherished fundamental values, without the slightest qualm of conscience. It may be caused by a chemical imbalance in the brain or it may just be the result of homiletic anesthesia. However, whatever its cause may be, Catholics have it down to a science.

Lutherans don't, at least the Lutherans I know. They have an officially approved hymnal. They are very careful not to sing anything they do not believe. They seem to be laboring under the delusion that what is sung has importance. They seem to think that they are passing on things that they believe in their music. Salvation comes by faith, and faith by hearing. They generally sing with great gusto, because their role in the worship service is to proclaim their faith. Words and music are important to them. They are almost sacramental. They bring salvation. Everyone knows it, and, therefore, everyone sings. It would never occur to a Missouri Synod Lutheran to sing a hymn of ambiguous theological content. Sacred music is simply too much of a faith statement to become insignificant.

I know almost nothing about music. I am tone deaf and unable to read music. Therefore, I spend an inordinate amount of time thinking about the meaning of the words of songs. Judging by the theological content of many of the songs used during the Eucharist, I must be one of the few dinosaurs in America to care about the meaning of words Catholics sing.

Contemporary Catholic hymns can be divided into several categories. First, there are songs that sound good but are politically incorrect. They provide one of the primary battlegrounds in the gender wars. Familiar songs that make use of *man* or *men* are sometimes updated by substituting *person* or *people*. When they obviously begin to sound silly, they are sometimes fixed by adding whole new verses to balance offending lyrics. *Faith of our Fathers* is corrected by singing a rousing, newly composed verse which begins, *Faith of our Mothers...* Of course, whole new pieces of music are sometimes composed to counter the perception of a universal masculine gender bias. *For All the Faithful Women* is sung to the tune of *The Church's One Foundation*. It is not particularly profound, but it does mention a lot of women, and I guess that is the point.

It would be unfair to limit musical revisionism to gender issues. Patriotic songs are sometimes changed to reflect such things as ecological issues, racial justice, world peace, and the dangers of jingoism. I once heard a version of *America* that was so introspective and critical that it almost made me want to burn the flag. I had the distinct impression that the *thoroughfare for freedom* went directly over the bleeding bodies of Native American children. I had always like the verse that ended, "...God mend thine every flaw, confirm thy soul in self control, thy liberty in law." I considered that a patriotic examination of conscience. It seemed to me that the congregation was asking pardon for mistakes and the lack of national self-control, and requesting divine help in correcting those problems.

All-in-all, I have always considered *America* to be a rather moderate piece of patriotic music that recognized God's generosity to America and the corresponding responsibility imposed by the wealth of this country to be used in accord with the wisdom and will of God. I really do not know why this particular piece of music had to be *fixed*. In the end, it really didn't matter. The politically correct verses were so unfamiliar that the congregation reverted to mousy mouthing of the now alien hymn. One person could hardly hear what the person next to him was singing. *America the Beautiful, God Bless America,* and *The Battle* (God forbid!) *Hymn of the Republic* all have politically correct versions. All are clumsy, unfamiliar, pointless, and unsingable, which may be the real point.

Second, there are songs familiar in the Protestant tradition which are real classics. They sound good and are known to most Americans regardless of denominational affiliation. I am reasonably certain that the preponderance of American Moslems and Jews are as familiar with *Amazing Grace* as Catholics or Presbyterians. The problem is that this song presents a Calvinist anthropology, which is totally inconsistent with Catholicism. That probably does not bother many people at mass. Some attempts have been made to baptize the hymn Catholic. *A wretch like me* is sometimes replaced with the more Catholic sounding *saved and set me free. A wretch like me* conjures up images of Luther's dung hill covered with snow, or Calvin's *massa damnata,* or even Jonathan Edward's loathsome sinner dangling from the hand of an angry God, on a single spider wed, over the fiery pit of hell. The truth is that Catholics do not view human beings as wretches. The Catholic Church proclaims the dignity of baptized people almost to an extreme. The Catholic Church believes that there are no bad people on earth. Everyone, even the worst mass murderer to have ever lived, is a good person, who sometimes does bad things. No one is radically predestined to be eternally lost.

Conversion is possible for every human being. Perhaps, that, more than anything else, has been the motivating factor for the incredible missionary fervor of Catholicism. It has never been the Catholic view that any race or group of people is so miserable or unsuitable for membership in the Church that they should not be evangelized. There are no damned masses of wretches living on earth, who, by that very fact, deserve the poverty and misery they endure. They are not wretches and I am not a wretch.

Not only that, the world is not a wretched place. The Catholic understanding of creation assumes that everyone and everything that God made is good.

I was once invited to explain the Catholic faith to a neighboring Baptist congregation. After my short presentation, I opened the program for questions from the audience. An elderly lady, one I recognized around town, began a series of questions:

"Brother, you Catholics drink alcohol, don't you?"

"Yes, ma'am, many Catholics do drink alcohol, and I'm one of 'em."

"Now, doesn't the bible say that we shouldn't get drunk?"

"Yes, ma'am, it does."

"Brother John, if you drink six beers, will you be drunk?"

"No, ma'am, I would not. But I still wouldn't drive a car. Eight beers would do the trick, though."

"Then, if you are drunk after eight beers—you are one eighth drunk after drinking one beer. So, it's a sin to drink one beer."

That line of thought fascinated me. I decided to give it a try myself.

"Ma'am, do you like to eat steak?"

"I like it, but with my false teeth, I can't have it."

"Nevertheless, if you ate six steaks—went off and vomited them up and then ate two more, would that be the sin of gluttony?"

"It sure would, Brother!"

"Then if you are a glutton after eating eight steaks—you are one eighth a glutton after eating one steak. So, eating steak is a sin. Is that right?"

The conversation did not end with that, but I seemed to have gained more respect with that congregation, when it became clear that I could speak their language. What we had been discussing was not a frivolous exercise in semantics. It was the fundamental difference between two worldviews. One proposed that things and people could be evil in themselves, wretched. The other maintained that no one and nothing is, fundamentally, evil

Beer is not evil in the Catholic worldview. To be sure, misusing it by becoming drunk is wrong—but beer is not an evil thing, any more than steak is evil. My Baptist brothers and sisters may believe that beer is the devil's brew and an evil poison. One approach to creation is Calvinist, and the other is Catholic. *Amazing Grace* proclaims, perfectly, the Calvinist conception of created matter. It's a nice song, but it does not reflect the faith of Catholics.

Protestants have wonderful hymns. Many can be enjoyed and sung by any lover of Jesus, in any church. *His Eye is on the Sparrow* and *The Old Rugged Cross* have always been among my favorites. Others express distinctly Protestant theology. There is nothing wrong with them as long as they are in a Protestant context. Unfortunately, they are often such good pieces of music that they are now familiar at mass. One of my favorite eyebrow raisers is a little tune called *Look Beyond*. Its words proclaim, "Look beyond the bread you eat, see your Savior and your Lord." I actually enjoy this song. It is a nice piece of music and the words are not clumsy or forced. However, I can not help asking, "Why should I look beyond the Bread I eat? I am Catholic. I believe that the bread becomes the living body, blood, soul and divinity of Jesus. I do not believe that it remains bread, and that Jesus enters into it. Why, then, would I want to look beyond the Bread, or for that matter, the Cup—which, I assume is a poetic expression for the Precious Blood?"

The third group of songs which catches my attention is kiddy hymns. These often express the most basic and profound articles of faith. They have been used for centuries to lay the foundation for a faith which will one day grow to maturity based on just these principles. My favorite kiddy song that expresses something that is antithetical to the things Catholics believe is *His Banner Over Me is Wuve* (sometimes pronounced *love*). It contains the line, "Peter built the Church on the rock of our faith, His banner over me is *wuve*." The only problem with this is that it denies what we believe about how the Church was established and what role Peter played in that foundation. We, as Catholics, believe that Jesus established His Church on Simon, when he was the first apostle to proclaim Jesus as the Messiah. Jesus then changed his name to Peter and told him that He would build His Church on the Rock, Peter, and the gates of hell would not prevail against it. This Scripture is the rationale for papal primacy. That is precisely what the verse in *His Banner...* was originally written to counter. The verse accurately proclaims a perfectly good Protestant ecclesiology, which happens to be totally inconsistent with Catholic dogma.

Now, little kids aren't going to know beans about papal primacy. They are not going to go through any mental gymnastics to reconcile building the Church on our faith, with the role of Peter among the apostles. What will stick in their minds is a catchy little verse. At some distant time, someone, or more probably a pair of people, will knock on an adult's door to explain Christianity to them. There will be a statue of Mary in the front yard and a crucifix on the living room wall. The Catholic Bible on top of the television will have drying leaves pressed in it by the fourth grader attending the local Catholic school.

The door-to-door evangelist will eventually get around to asking "Don't you know that Jesus built the Church on the rock of our faith? Then why do you care what an old man, in a white dress, living in Rome thinks about anything?" At that moment, the homeowner will quietly hum one of his old childhood favorites, "Jesus built the Church on the rock of our faith, His banner over me is wuve."

The fourth group of songs is the few perfectly good songs that have, finally, become familiar enough to most Catholics that they form the tiny core of musical pieces that are committed to memory. *I am the Bread of Life* immediately comes to mind.

Catholics are widely denounced because they will not sing. However, these few songs are popular enough to have become familiar to people. *Be not afraid* is another one of these. Just when the congregation is revved up and really into it, the familiar verses sometimes dissolve into unfamiliar rewrites that muzzle worshipers more than a stewardship video. The old thunderous, "And He will raise him up! And He will raise him up! And he will raise him up, on the last day!" Suddenly becomes a mousy and unfamiliar, "And He will raise *you* up..." Worshipers stare blankly at each other, with a look that says, "I thought I knew the words to that one, but I guess not." The singing almost stops and the former thunder is reduced to a squeak, and the local liturgists all have one more example, proving that Catholics just won't sing, no matter how hard they are prodded.

Then, there are the really bad songs. They are in a class all by themselves. They range from popular rock-and-roll songs with new lyrics to the first efforts of budding composers. They may be catchy but that is only because they have the elegance of deep-fried chicken jingles. My suspicion is that every Catholic in America has his own list of these adorable little ditties. I see little value in providing my own. It would simply insult people who have an occasional desire to overdose on bubble gum.

I don't want to be too harsh on liturgical music. The task before composers and liturgists is monumental. An entire body of sacred music has to be reestablished that expresses the faith of a whole people. It has to teach, inspire, and unite communities where incredible diversity is as close as the next pew. New classics have to be invented. In all of this, mistakes are inevitable.

Nevertheless, words have meaning. Singing things that are opposed to the basic tenets of our faith, or placing faith statements in a subordinate position to culturally conditioned stands on social justice, invites destructive ambiguity into liturgical worship. In this *differences really don't matter* context, the crucifix might more appropriately be replaced with a yellow *smiley face*. I have absolutely no desire to witness the creation of a *Catholic Music Police*, but I care enough about the meaning of words to become the last Catholic American musical dinosaur. I can live with that.

Or, perhaps, I am not really alone. Maybe that is why so few Catholics sing. It could be that they are waiting for songs that are familiar enough to sing without a book: good music that really expresses what they believe. They don't want songs reformatted to make them more, dare I use the word, *relevant*. Until that happens, it is my best guess that Catholics will continue to squeak along, mouthing the mousy words of the latest piece of transitional *correctness* that they are browbeaten into attempting.

Someone's cryin', Lord, Kum-by-ya!

BONE 17

End Times

And there were voices, and thunders, and lightnings;
And there was a great earthquake,
such as was not since men were upon the earth,
so mighty an earthquake, and so great.

—Revelation 16:18

St. Joseph of Apple Creek Church was built on the New Madrid fault. Everyone knew that the *big one* could come at any time. When a professor from nearby Southeastern Missouri University claimed an earthquake would take place in early December of 1989, most local people paid attention.

Gus and Mae Buchheit built a little piece of paradise about three miles west of the Church. They had transformed an old barn into a woodworking shop, where Gus made most of their furniture.

They surrounded their pond with pine trees obtained from the local conservation department. The pond was stocked with huge catfish and really large hybrid bluegill. They treated their fish as pets. Only their grandchildren and the parish priest were allowed to fish the pond.

I enjoyed catching the Buchheit fish. It was a lot like fishing in a large fishbowl. When I threw my line in the water, it churned with fish fighting to bite my hook. Within minutes, I always caught enough fish for several meals. My freezer was full.

It was late in the evening. I was beginning to feel guilty about the number of fish I was taking from the Buchheit's pond. I decided to take home what I had, and give that pond a rest. Tomorrow, I would visit Grandma Ponder's pond. It's good to be the priest!

The following morning there was an all-school mass at Apple Creek. Shortly before the Preface to the Eucharistic Prayer, the building began to vibrate. There was a powerful sound like an enormous truck rumbling past the Church. But this was no truck. It was the earth moving beneath us!

The brick Church was over one hundred years old. It had a high traditional ceiling. The sound of the tremor was amplified in the open space above our heads.

My first concern was to prevent the children from attempting to run out of the building. I did not know how strong the tremor would be. However, I feared trampled children, piled at the doors of our Church.

The children were all standing. I invited them to kneel, and I offered a prayer for our deliverance from the quake. The vibration and the sound ended at the exact moment that I ended the prayer. I signaled the children to stand, and we continued our mass.

That did it! Now the whole area started planning for the *big one*. Members of the national news media began paying more attention to Dr. Iben Browning's prediction of a December 3rd earthquake along the New Madrid fault.

The only real harm done by our little tremor was at the Buchheit's. The morning of our little quake, every drop of water and every fish in the pond disappeared down the newly opened sinkhole. Theresa Meyer, our oldest living parishioner at one hundred and two, remembered something like that happening ninety years earlier. Her brothers had been fishing in a farm pond when a similar earthquake had struck. They had been so frightened by the whole affair that they had jumped out of their wooden shoes, to run faster for home. I spent just a moment chastising myself for not catching more of their fish the previous evening.

An attitude of *"it might just happen!"* began to spread. Ordinarily levelheaded people were beginning to speculate about the chances of Dr. Browning being right. Someone noticed that December was the twelfth month. The *big one* was predicted for the third day, because of a full moon with corresponding high tides—remember, Missouri is about as far from tides as a person can get and still be in the United States. *What if* the *big one* came at five minutes after four in the morning? *What if* it registered 6.7 on the Richter Scale? It was 1989. All that adds up to month, 12; day, 3; 4:05 a.m.; a 6.7 quake; in '89. 1-2-3-4-5-6-7-8-9, *could it be Satan?*

I really did not want to address this, at all. However, when the local public schools announced that they would be closed on December 3rd, and the Catholic and Lutheran Schools, in town, followed their example, a decision had to be made. Even our neighbors at St. Maurus announced that their tiny school would close on the fateful day.

Things were beginning to get out of hand. One member of the parish bought four derelict refrigerators and filled them with can goods and dried food. They were located at the four corners of his farm, so that at least a couple of them would survive the *big one!* Most of the people of the parish were beginning to store up extra food and water. Several admitted to stocking up on ammunition! There were daily calls to the rectory inquiring about school on December 3rd.

I called an emergency meeting of the Parish Council, and expressed my concern that the community was becoming paranoid and self-concerned. I asked the Council to prepare a plan for meeting the needs of all our neighbors in the event of any emergency—fire, flood, tornado, or earthquake. I invited the Council to become a voice of stability and calm. Emergency routes were discussed. Procedures for centralizing food and water were considered. Those with two-way radios in their cars and trucks established local communication networks. A systematic plan for checking on neighbors was drawn up.

It was obvious that the teachers in the grade school were still concerned. The teachers insisted that gallon jugs of water be stored in every classroom. There was enough dried and canned food in the school pantry to feed the children for several days. Our first aid box was updated.

At the insistence of the faculty, I called the architect, and asked about the effect of an earthquake on our school building. I learned that, in the event of a medium strength earthquake, our school building, less than ten years old, was probably one of the least dangerous buildings in the area.

The Sunday before the big day, I announced at all the masses that there would be school on December 3rd. I also asked the people to try to calm down.

The national media was beginning to poke fun at us. Network news teams were moving into New Madrid, more to record the local hysteria than the potential earthquake. We were all beginning to look like a bunch of buffoons.

My decision to keep the school open actually had more to do with calming the potentially dangerous situation that was developing. I halfway expected to pick up the local newspaper on December 4th and read about the tragic shooting of some poor soul who just happened to wander too close to one of those abandoned refrigerators full of food.

I had certificates printed, with a picture of a school in the center. The certificate read "I fought ignorance. I attended School on 1-2-3-4-5-6-7-8-9." Only two children stayed home that day, both from the same family. I signed each certificate and presented one to every child who came to school.

Of course, nothing happened. In the days that followed most people tried to forget how silly we looked.

In a few weeks, the world will mark the 2000th anniversary of the birth of Jesus Christ. That day will usher in a Holy Year. I suppose that the three zeros after the numeral, two are responsible for the panic in supermarket tabloid headlines. They are growing more ridiculous by the day. Apparently, some people are *hearing* things, and *seeing* things, and *getting ready* for the *Great Period of Tribulation* mentioned in the bible.

On the day the world marks the anniversary of the first coming of Our Lord and Savior, thousands, perhaps hundreds of thousands, of frightened people will be hiding in their basements with Spam and candles. Some will have guns and ammunition for protection. My guess is that a few will commit suicide. More of them will experience the trauma of panic, bordering on terror.

I read the same bible as all of these people. Mine says, "You know not the hour or the day." When I share that verse with those already whipped into near hysteria, I hear: "Yes, we will not know the hour or the day, but that doesn't mean we won't know the week or the month!"

There are not many things I hate worse than using the Bible to proof text an argument. I do so only because it is the only way to address these issues on their home court. The words of Jesus recorded in the seventeenth chapter of Luke's Gospel address those who see the approaching End Time in every earthquake and famine. When asked about the establishment of the Kingdom of God Jesus replied, "You cannot tell by careful watching when the reign of God will come. Neither is it a matter of reporting that it is 'here' or 'there.' The reign of God is already in your midst." He goes on to speak about the *Day of the Son of Man* in apocalyptic terms. The point is to be always ready to welcome Him. Never pass up an opportunity to do good or to repent of evil. Then the End Time will always look like the approaching answer to a fond prayer.

In the mean time, if it will reassure frightened people, I'm ready to refill the gallon milk jugs with water and update the first aid kit, but frankly, I've been here before. I plan to celebrate the Y2K moment, *the night of the really big one,* with a beer and a good night's sleep.

I'm reminded of the sign in a religious bookstore window. The owner of the store had come to believe that the world would end on a particular day in 1990. The sign read, "This store will be closed tomorrow, so that our employees can spend the last day on earth with their families. We'll be open the following day."

What more could I add to that?

Bones of Contention

CONCLUSION

No Bones About It

Here's to You,
And Here's to Me;
If We Should Ever Disagree,
Well, Here's to Me!
—Old toast

So, what's the point? Anyone can sit back and take pot shots at things that are important to other people. Who am I to think that my opinions are so orthodox, that I have the right to laugh at the passionate causes of sisters and brothers in the faith?

The truth is that members of the Church have made a lot of mistakes. This is the real news flash of every age.

The Black Death was not the beginning of the End Times. The Franciscan and Dominican mendicant movements of the thirteenth century did not usher in the Age of the Spirit, with a corresponding *All New and Improved Third Testament of Sacred Scripture.* The discovery of Mexico City was not the finding of the New Jerusalem. In my own time, 1960 did not produce the dreaded *Secret of Fatima,* with its imagined promise of End Time doom. Although, I have to admit that my pastor did manage to scare me into a few extra rosaries with stories of swooning popes who had read the dreaded promise of divine retribution dictated at Fatima by the Blessed Mother to Lucia.

I was part of the generation that skipped lunch during the Cuban Missile Crisis to make a quick confession—the one and only time the line for confession stretched out of the Mercy High School chapel, halfway down the hall. That was also the day that the school had its one and only atomic war drill. I was assigned a place in the first floor hall. The school basement was for seniors. I still don't know why they were more deserving of being buried under the radioactive rubble than I was.

Well, we're all still here. Perhaps, Jesus will come back today. Maybe those folks who will spend New Year's Eve, 1999, in their basements, with a can of Spam and a candle, will see the beginning of the *Great Period of Tribulation*, but I really doubt it.

The world, especially during this segment of its history, is a confusing place. Americans are so used to instant everything that we are impatient with the pace of any change. We expect all injustices to be overcome in our lifetime. We want the revolutionary reforms of the Second Vatican Council to be implemented immediately, or more accurately, we want them in place thirty years ago. Some people believe that the world has already outgrown them.

It took nearly five hundred years for the faith of Nicea to completely triumph over Arianism. The Council of Chalcedon is still not universally accepted by all Christians. The Council of Florence has yet to succeed in ending the now thousand year division between the Orthodox and the Catholic Church. The Council of Trent was in session for eighteen years. It was unable to end the divisions in western Christendom. Those divisions are still with us and seem to be as difficult to heal as they were nearly five hundred years ago.

So, we have had a great Church Council. It opened up more than a few windows. It has made us all think. Some of us see things that need correction; others see things of beauty and stability in danger of slipping away. Everyone has an agenda. Some want faster change; others want to slow things down; still others want to turn back the clock. There is even talk in some circles of a *Third* Vatican Council.

It will take as long for this period of innovation and reform to become established as it has in any other historical period. I suggest that we all just get comfortable with that. Mistakes will be made, and the Church will have to respond to them. It is not an absolute requirement that we grind each other up in the process.

A religious sister of considerable stature headed up the Catholic School System in a major mid-western archdiocese all through the seventies and eighties. Toward the end of her tenure she had a standard stump speech. It began by recognizing that the Catholic schools stopped teaching religion in the late sixties and replaced it with values clarification and pop psychology. Sister claimed that she knew this to be true because she taught what passed for religion at that time, and it was not really religion at all.

I have heard that talk several times. I think it is one of the best I have ever heard. But what of those crusty old pastors who said the same thing back when it was happening? Most of them were pigeon-holed as obstructionist reactionaries, who were unable to adapt to the new changes ushered in by the Second Vatican Council.

Some were precisely that. However, others were sincere in believing that the faith was no longer being taught to a whole generation. In the early days of the renewal, many sincere pastors were brushed aside and ignored. A number of them lost everything because they were painted with the same brush as the obstructionists.

Now, it is fashionable to admit that they may have had a point. That's nice! The Church has recently gotten around to apologizing for the condemnation of Galileo, the persecution of the Jews, and its role in the shattering of Christian unity. Perhaps it is time to apologize to all of those wounded in the early liturgical and catechetical wars. But just once, wouldn't it be nice to get it right going into a situation.

The present age is unsettled. It is the lot of every Catholic to search for new ways to make the faith understandable and attractive—which is still the Great Commission: go forth and baptize *all* nations. This period of turmoil will not be shortened by bad humor or mean spiritedness. It is all right to laugh at ourselves. It is all right to point out inconsistencies in a light-hearted way, as long as that does not descend into ridicule. It is even all right to listen to things that are wrong, simply out of respect for those who believe them, without reducing our faith to disconnected individual opinion.

Sacred Tradition, often misrepresented as the worship of the status quo, is more than the historical account of what has or has not happened. It is the lived experience of the Holy Spirit working within human history. *New* is not a four-letter word! Innovation is not the enemy. There has to be room to probe the boundaries and make mistakes. That is the only way that the frontier of ignorance is pushed back. However, the new discoveries have to rest on the foundation laid by the Christ event.

Ideas make progress in the Church by building on the Truth, not by ripping it up and replacing it. The Gospel of Christ must become new in this age, but it must also be rooted in an historical event memorialized as *year one*. For the proclaimed faith of the third millenium to be an expression of Christ's Gospel, it has to be part of all that has been proclaimed by the Church up to this present age. It cannot be an entirely new invention. In fact, it is simply the newest layer of the *onion*. The humbling truth is that history records practically every controversy and issue discussed in the contemporary Church. Few ideas are entirely new. Most challenges to elements of the Christian faith have been decided dozens of times, and with great consistency, by local synods or Ecumenical Councils.

An expression of the Christian faith for the new millenium should not be based only on popular contemporary conceptions of right or wrong— the rationale for slavery and genocide has sometimes rested on such a premise. Faith is broader than that. Something of the eternal has to lift it up.

My best guess is that we are all in this world for the long haul. Most of us seek real answers to real problems. Simplistic, memorized responses to straightjacketed questions are of little use in navigating the complexities of daily life. I wish the world were a simpler place in which to live, but wishing it to be uncomplicated does little good. The world has to be confronted as it is, or religious faith becomes a fairy tale.

While we are all working to discover new ways to express Eternal Truth, we could growl less, bite less, and be a little more willing to share the *bones of contention*. In more concrete terms: people, whether you are a traditionalist, feminist, male chauvinist, homophobe, dogmatist, legalist, charismatic, liberal, conservative, moderate, political activist, or a liturgist—just lighten up!